ROUMANIAN FAIRY TALES AND LEGENDS

Dedicated by Permission

TO HER MAJESTY

QUEEN ELIZABETH

OF

ROUMANIA.

PREFACE.

THE literature of Roumania is so little known in England, that I have ventured to translate, and bring before the public, some of the popular *Basme* (tales) and legends of the country.

I have kept to the original text as strictly as possible, but some of the idioms are untranslatable.

Of the Poets, I have given no specimen, though there are many of recognised talent.

A volume of Roumanian poems has just been put into the German tongue, by the August Lady who permits me to dedicate this small effort to her, and who is the patron of every good work.

By its bravery, and its stedfast perseverance in its onward path, ROUMANIA has raised itself into a KINGDOM; and I have thought it well to insert in this little book "The Martyrdom of Brancovan," and the Spartan courage of the "Mother of Stefan the Great," to shew of what blood the true sons and daughters of Roumania are made.

E. B. M.
BUCHAREST.
April, 1881.

CONTENTS

FAIRY TALES.

THE SLIPPERS OF THE TWELVE PRINCESSES. 17
THE UNGRATEFUL WOOD-CUTTER. 30
THE HERMIT'S FOUNDLING WITH THE GOLDEN HAIR. 34
THE DAUGHTER OF THE ROSE. 44
THE TWELVE-HEADED GRIFFIN. 48
VASILICA THE BRAVE. 55
"HANDSOME IS AS HANDSOME DOES." 70
THE FISHERMAN AND THE BOYARD'S DAUGHTER. 76

LEGENDS.

MANOLI. 83
THE FORTRESS OF POINARII. 89
THE GENTLE SHEPHERD. 94

HISTORIC TALES.

DEATH OF CONSTANTIN II. BRANCOVAN. 99
THE MOTHER OF STEPHEN THE GREAT. 103

LIST OF ILLUSTRATIONS

QUEEN ELIZABETH OF ROUMANIA...2
JONICA'S DREAM 18
FIGHT OF HORSE AND DRAGON.. 57
MONASTERY OF ARGISCH.. 83

FAIRY TALES.

THE SLIPPERS OF
THE TWELVE PRINCESSES.

I.

ONCE on a time, in the good old times, there lived a cow-herd, who had neither father nor mother. He was called Jonica, that is to say Johnnie, but people had given him the name of *Gura Casca* (open mouth) because when he led his cows to pasture, he bellowed at every thing which he met on the way. Otherwise he was really a very pretty boy, his face was fair, and his eyes as blue as a morsel of the sky, with hair curling, and as yellow as the rays of the Sun. The young girls of the village teased him sadly. "Hé! Hé! Jonica, where are you going with your open mouth"? "What does that matter to you"? he would reply tranquilly, and pass on his way. Though only a cow-herd, he was sufficiently proud of his good looks, and he knew quite well the difference between beauty and ugliness, so the young peasant girls with their faces and throats tanned by the sun, their large hands red and cracked, their feet shod in "opinci" (a rough sort of sandal) or other common leather, were not at all to his mind.

He had heard tell, that, down there, a long way off, in the towns, the young girls were quite different; that they had throats as white as alabaster, pink cheeks, delicate and soft hands, their small feet covered by satin slippers, that in short they were clad in robes of silk and gold, and were called Princesses. So that, while his comrades only sought to please some rustic villager, he dreamed, neither more nor less, that he should marry a Princess.

One noon-day in the middle of August, when the sun was so scorching that even the flies did not know where to put themselves, Jonica sat down under the shadow of an oak to eat his *mammaliga* (thick Indian meal porridge) and a morsel of sheep's milk cheese; seeing that his flock was lying peaceably about, he stretched himself at fall length, and was soon asleep.

He had a charming dream! a *Zina*, a fairy, appeared to him, beautiful as the day, fresh as a rose,

JONICA'S DREAM

and clad in a robe sparkling with diamonds. She said to him—

"There is a country where precious stones grow; go to the Court of the Emperor who reigns there, and you will marry a Princess."

In the evening, when he took his cows back to the stable, Jonica recounted his dream to several of his friends, who freely laughed at him. But the words of the Zina had such an influence on him, that he laughed himself at the ridicule of which he was the object.

The next day, at the same hour, and the same place, our cow-herd came to take his siesta. He had the same dream; and the same fairy, more radiant than ever, appeared again to him, and repeated: "There is a country where precious stones grow; go to the Court of the Emperor who reigns there and you will marry a Princess."

Jonica again repeated his dream, and it was again turned into ridicule.

"What does it matter to me," said Jonica, "if they laugh! I know one thing, that if that fairy appears again to me, I'll follow her advice."

On the following day he had the same dream, he got up joyfully, and in the evening they heard him in the village singing: "I quit the cows and calves, for I am going to marry the daughter of an Emperor."

His master, who overheard him, became thoughtful, but Jonica said to him, "You may do, and think as you like, but it is decided! I am going away!" He began to make his preparations, and in the morning he left.

The people of the village held their sides with laughing, when they saw him with his little bundle on a stick, slung across his shoulder, descend the hill, traverse the plain, and then slowly disappear, in the dim distance.

III.

In those days, people did say that there was really a country where precious stones grew, as grass, plants, and flowers grow in other places. It was said that the Emperor of these parts had twelve daughters—twelve Princesses, the one prettier than the other, but all as proud as they were beautiful. It was said also, that they only went to sleep at sunrise, and got up at mid-day.

They lived altogether in one large room of the Palace, and slept in beds of gold, encrusted with flowers of diamonds and emeralds.

When the Princesses retired in the evening, the nine doors of their apartment were locked outside with nine padlocks. It was impossible for them to get out, and yet each night something very extraordinary took place.

The satin slippers of the twelve Princesses, were literally worn out each morning. One might have thought that the daughters of the Emperor had danced all night. When they were questioned, they declared that they knew nothing, and could understand nothing about it. No one could explain this strange fact, for, notwithstanding the greatest watchfulness, not the least noise had ever been heard in the chamber of the Princesses, after they had retired to rest.

The Emperor, their father, was most perplexed, and determined, at any price, to penetrate this mystery. He had a trumpet sounded, and it was published throughout all the country, that if any one succeeded in finding out, by what means his daughters, the Princesses, wore out their slippers in a single night, he might choose from amongst them, his wife. At this news, a great number of Emperors' sons, and Kings' sons, presented themselves to explore this adventure. They hid themselves behind a great curtain in the chamber of the Princesses. But once there, no one ever heard any more of them, and they never re-appeared.

Our Jonica, who arrived just then at the Court of the Emperor, heard talk of all these matters, and succeeded in being taken into the service of one of the Imperial Gardeners, who) had been obliged to send away one of his best helps. His new master did not find him very intelligent, but he was convinced that his curling light hair and good looks, would make him acceptable to the Princesses.

Thus his daily duty, then, was each morning to present a bouquet to the daughters of the Emperor. Jonica posted himself at their door, at the hour of their awakening, and as each came forth, he presented her with a bouquet. They found the flowers very beautiful, but disdained to cast a look or smile on poor Jonica, who remained there more than ever, *Gura Casca*, open-mouthed.

Lina, alone, the youngest, the most graceful, and the prettiest of the Princesses, let fall by hazard on him, a look as soft as velvet. "Ah! my sisters," cried she, "how good looking our young gardener is!"

They burst into mocking laughter, and the eldest remarked to Lina, that it was unbecoming a Princess to lower her eyes to a valet. Nevertheless, Jonica intoxicated by the looks and the beauty of Lina, thought of the promise of the Emperor, and it entered into his head to try and discover the mystery of the slippers. He did not mention it to any one though, for he was afraid that the Emperor might hear of it, be angry, and have him driven away from Court, as a punishment for his audacity.

IV.

While these thoughts were passing through his brain, Jonica dreamed again of the fairy with the sparkling robe. She held in her right hand two small laurel branches, one was as red as a cherry, and the other like a rose; in her left hand was a little golden spade, a watering can of the same metal, and a silken veil.

She gave all these to Jonica, saying, "Plant these two laurels in large boxes, turn over the earth with this spade, water them with this watering-can, and wipe them with this silken veil. When they have grown three feet high, say to each separately, "Beautiful laurels, with a golden spade I have dug you, with a golden watering-can I have watered you, and with a silken veil I have wiped you." "This said, you can ask anything you wish, and it will be accorded you." When Jonica awoke he found the two laurels and the other objects on the table, and fell on his knees to thank the good fairy. He at once began to carry out her instructions. The shrubs grew rapidly, and when they had attained the necessary height, he went to the cherry laurel, and said:

"Beautiful cherry laurel, with a golden spade I have dug you, with a golden can I have watered you, with a silken veil I have wiped you; grant me in exchange, the gift of becoming invisible whenever I desire." Immediately he saw grow out from the laurel, a beautiful white flower. He gathered it, placed it in his button-hole, and at once became invisible.

When night arrived, the Princesses went up to their bedroom, and Jonica, bare-footed, so as to make no noise, glided up behind them, and hid himself underneath one of the twelve beds.

Then, instead of preparing themselves to go to bed, each of the Princesses opened a wardrobe, and took out their richest dresses and finest jewels. Each assisting the other, they dressed *en grande toilette*. Jonica could see nothing from his hiding place, but he heard them laugh, and dance with joy. The eldest, who seemed to have great authority over them, hurried them, and kept exclaiming: "Be quick, my sisters, our dancers are dying of impatience." At the end of an hour, the laughing and talking ceased. Jonica carefully put out his head, and saw that the Princesses were dressed like fairies. They wore quite new satin slippers, and held in their hands the bouquets which he had offered to them in the morning.

They placed themselves one behind the other, and the eldest who was at the head, struck three blows in a peculiar manner, on a certain part of the wall. A door quite invisible opened, and the Princesses disappeared.

Jonica followed them noiselessly, but by accident he placed his foot on the train of the Princess Lina. "There is some one behind me," she cried, "some one trod on my dress." The eldest turned round quickly, but seeing no one, exclaimed, "how foolish you are Lina, you must have caught it against a nail."

The twelve daughters of the Emperor, descended, and descended, and descended until they arrived at an underground passage, at the end of which was an iron door with a strong bolt.

The eldest opened this, and then they found themselves in an enchanted bower, where the leaves of the trees were in silver, and sparkled in the moonlight. They walked on until they came to a second bower, and here the trees had golden leaves; still on, and then a third bower, where the leaves were of emeralds and rubies and diamonds, and their rays were so bright that one might have thought it was full daylight. The princesses continued their walk, and (Jonica still following), arrived soon on the borders of a large lake.

On this lake were twelve boats, and in each boat one of the lost sons of an Emperor, who, oar in hand, each waited for a Princess. Jonica took his place in the boat of the Princess Lina. The boat, being more heavily laden, could not float so quickly as the others, and so was always behind. "I do not know," said Lina to her cavalier, "why we do not go so quickly as at other times, what can be the matter?"

"I do not understand it either," said the Emperor's son, "for I row with all my force."

On the other side of the lake the little gardener perceived a beautiful palace, illuminated *a giorno*, and heard harmonious sounds of violins, trumpets and cymbals. The Emperors' sons each having a Princess on his arm entered the palace, and after them came Jonica into a saloon lighted by ten lustres.

The walls were immense mirrors, in gold frames set with precious stones. On a centre table a massive golden vase contained an enormous bouquet of flowers which gave forth an exquisite perfume. Poor Jonica was literally dazed and petrified by the sight of so much splendour. When able to look at, and admire the Princesses in the midst of this dazzling light, he lost his wits completely, and looked so ardently with his eyes, that one would have thought that he wished to taste them also with his mouth. Some were fair, some were brown, and nearly all of them had let fall their beautiful hair down their pretty white shoulders. Never, even in his dreams, had the poor boy seen such enchanteresses.

But amongst them all, and above all, it was Lina, who seemed to him the most graceful, the most beautiful, thee most intoxicating, with her dark eyes and long-hair—the shade of a raven's wing. And with what fire she danced! leaning on the shoulder of her cavalier, Lina turned as light as a spindle. Her face was flushed, her eyes shone like two stars, and it was evident that dancing was her great delight.

Poor Jonica let fall envious looks on the Emperors' sons, and heartily regretted not to be on the same footing, so that he also might have had the right to be cavalier to such beautiful young creatures. All these dancers, to the number of fifty, were Emperors' sons who had tried to discover the secret of the Princesses.

These latter had enticed them to a midnight expedition, and had given them to drink at table, an enchanted beverage, which had frozen their blood, killed in them every sentiment of love, every remembrance, or worldly desire, leaving them only the ardent pleasure of the dance, in the bosom of this splendid palace, become henceforth their eternal habitation.

VI.

The Princesses danced until their white satin slippers were in holes, until the cock had crowed three times. Then the music ceased, black slaves arranged a princely table, which was instantaneously filled with the most succulent meats, and the rarest and most exquisite wines. Each one took his place, and ate and drank at his ease, excepting our poor *Gusa Casca*, who had to content himself with feasting his eyes alone. When the repast was over, the Princesses re-entered their boat, and Jonica who followed them step by step, arrived with them in the wood with the silver leaves.

There, to prove to himself, and to prove also to others, that what he had seen was no dream, Jonica broke off a branch of the tree with the beautiful leaves. The noise which he made, caused Lina to turn round. "What can that be?" said she to her sisters. "Probably," said the eldest, it is the rustling amongst the branches of some bird, that has its nest in one of the towers of the Palace." Jonica then got in advance of the Princesses, and mounted rapidly to their chamber, opened the window, and glided silently along the trellis which covered the wall, and began his daily work.

While preparing the flowers for the Princesses, he hid the branch of Silver Leaves in the bouquet destined for Lina.

Great was the astonishment of the young girl, who asked herself, in vain, how it was possible that the branch could have come there.

Without saying anything to her sisters, she went down into the garden, and there, under the shade of a large chestnut tree, she found the gardener. She had for the moment, a great mind to speak to him, but on reflection, thought it better to wait a little, and so passed on her way.

When evening arrived, the Princesses again returned to the Ball, Jonica followed them, and a second time entered Lina's boat. Again the Emperor's son complained of the labour required in rowing. "No doubt it is the heat which you feel," replied Lina. All passed as on the previous evening, but this time, on returning, Jonica broke off a branch of the Golden Leaves.

When the daily bouquets were distributed, the Princess Lina found, concealed in hers, the golden branch. Remaining a little behind her sisters, and showing the golden branch to Jonica, she asked, "From whence, hadst thou these leaves?"

"Your Highness knows quite well."

"So thou hast followed us?"

"Yes, Highness."

"And how didst thou manage that?"

"It is a secret."

"We did not see thee."

"I was invisible."

"At any rate, I see that thou hast penetrated the mystery. Speak of it to no one, and take this purse as the price of thy silence," and she throw to the poor boy, a purse of gold. "I do not sell my silence," said Jonica, with a haughtiness which astonished the Princess. "I know how to hold my tongue, without being paid for it." And he walked away, leaving the purse on the ground.

The three succeeding days, Lina neither saw nor heard anything particular, during their nocturnal excursions; but the fourth night, there was a distinct rustling in the wood of Diamond Leaves, and the next morning she found a Diamond Branch, hidden in her bouquet. Then she was fully convinced that the young gardener knew all their escapades, and calling him to her, she asked:

"Dost thou know the price, which the Emperor, our father, offers for the discovery of our secret?"

"I know it, Highness."

"Then why dost thou not go to him, and betray it?"

"I do not wish."

"Art thou afraid?"

"No, Highness."

"Then, why wilt thou not speak?"

Jonica looked up at her, his eyes full of expression, but did not reply.

VII.

While Lina was talking with the youth, her sisters were laughing at her, and when she came back they still went on with their ridicule, until she became quite red with anger.

"Thou canst marry him," said her sisters, "there is nothing to prevent; thou wilt be the gardener's wife, and thou wilt live in the cottage at the bottom of the garden. Thou canst help thy husband to draw the water from the fountain, and thou canst offer us our daily nosegays."

Lina became still more angry, and the weight of her anger fell on poor Jonica. When he again presented her with flowers, she took them with supreme indifference, and treated him with the greatest disdain. The poor fellow could not understand it, for he was always most respectful.

He never dared to look her full in the face, and yet she felt he was present with her all day long. At length, she came to the resolution to confide to her sisters all that she knew.

"What!" cried they, "this stupid boy has learned our secret, and thou hast kept it from us! We must, at once, absolutely get rid of him."

"By what means?"

"Have him stabbed, and thrown into a cave."

This was the usual way by which troublesome people were disposed of.

But Lina would not hear of this, saying that the poor boy had committed no fault.

"If you touch a hair of his head," she said, "I will go and confess all to our father the Emperor."

To tranquilise Lina, it was decided to get Jonica to go again to the Ball, and to make him drink the enchanted beverage, which would put him in the same state as the other Cavaliers. So they called the young gardener to them, and the eldest sister asked him by what means he had discovered their secret? but he would give them no answer. Then they informed him of the decision which they had come to respecting him. He replied, that he accepted it, and that he would drink willingly the enchanted beverage, so as to become the Cavalier of her whom he loved.

On the day fixed, wishing to have as fine clothes, and to be able to make as handsome presents as the Emperors' sons, Jonica went to the rose laurel, and said "my beautiful laurel, I have dug you with a golden spade, I have watered you with a golden watering can, I have wiped you with a silken veil, grant that, in one moment, I may be as richly dressed as an Emperor's son."

Immediately he saw a beautiful flower expand, and gathering it, he was at once clad in velvet as dark and soft as Lina's eyes, a toque to match, with an agraffe of diamonds, and a flower in his buttonhole. From being tanned and brown, his complexion became fair and fresh as an infant's and his beauty was marvellous. Even his common, vulgar manner changed completely, and any one might have thought him really an Emperor's son.

Thus metamorphosed, he presented himself before the Emperor, to ask his authority to try in his turn, to unravel the secret of the Princesses. He was so changed that the Emperor did not recognize him.

When the Princesses went back to their bedroom, Jonica was waiting for them behind the door. After their usual excursion, Jonica gave his arm to the eldest Princess, and afterwards danced with each of the sisters successively, and with so much dignity and grace, that they were all enchanted. When it was Lina's turn, he was in raptures; but he did not address a single word to her. While conducting her to her place, the Princess said to him, jokingly, "Being treated like an Emperor's son, thou must be in blissful happiness." "Never fear, Princess," replied he, "you shall not be a gardener's wife." Lina looked at him, half frightened, but he walked away, without waiting for her answer.

When the Princesses had once more danced until their slippers were in holes, the music ceased, the black slaves prepared the table as usual, and Jonica was placed at the right hand of the eldest Princess, and facing Lina. He was served with the most delicate meats, the choicest wines; compliments and praises were showered on him, but he was neither intoxicated by their wines, nor by their flatteries. Presently the eldest Princess made a sign, and one of the slaves came forward bearing a massive golden cup.

"This enchanted Palace has no longer any secrets for thee," cried the Princess to Jonica, "Let us drink to your triumph!" The young man casting tender glance at Lina, raised the cup to his lips.

"Do not drink it," she cried impetuously, "do not drink it, I would rather be a gardener's wife," and she began to weep.

Jonica threw the enchanted beverage over his shoulder, cleared the table, and fell on his knees at the feet of the Princess Lina. All the other Emperors' sons fell each at the feet of their respective Princesses, who choosing them for their husbands, held out their hands and raised them from the ground.

The charm was broken!

The twelve couples crossed the lake in boats, traversed the forests, passed through the cellar, and arrived at the Emperor's chamber. Jonica, with the golden cup in his hand, explained to him the mystery of the worn-out slippers. "God give thee life, young man," said the Emperor, "take thy choice from amongst my daughters."

"My choice has been made for a long time," said he, taking by the hand the Princess Lina, who blushed and could not look up.

IX.

The Princess Lina did not become a gardener's wife, for Jonica became a Prince. Before their marriage took place, Lina enquired of him, how he had discovered their secret. Jonica showed her the two laurels. Lina, like an intelligent woman, thought that Jonica would have too great an advantage over her, if he enjoyed the power which was given to him by possessing these shrubs, so she tore the laurels up by their roots and flung them into the fire.

A short time afterwards, the marriage took place with imperial splendour. It was followed by festivities which lasted three days and three nights, and the young people lived very happily together, to a good old age.

THE UNGRATEFUL WOOD-CUTTER.

ONCE on a time there lived in a village, a Woodcutter, so poor, so poor, that he had only his hatchet with which to gain bread for his wife and children. With difficulty could he earn six-pence a day, and it needed his wife and himself to rise early and go late to bed, so as to ensure them the coarsest food. Repose they had none.

"What am I to do?" said he, one day, "I am worn out with fatigue, my wife and children have nothing to eat, and I have no longer strength to hold my hatchet, to earn even bitter black bread for my family. Ah! it is very bad luck for the poor, when they are brought into this world."

While he was lamenting in this way, a voice called to him in a compassionate tone: "What are you complaining of?"

"Am I not likely to complain, when I have no food?" said he. "Go home," said the voice, "dig up the earth in the corner of your garden, and you will find under a dead branch, a treasure.

When the wood-cutter heard this, he threw himself on his knees, and cried out: "Master, how do you call yourself? who are you with so kind a heart?"

"My name is Merlin," said the voice."

"Ah! Master, God will bless you if you will come to my aid, and save a poor family from destitution."

"Go quickly," said the voice, "and in a year's time come back here, and give me an account of what you have done with the money you will find in the corner of the garden."

"Master, I will come in a year's time, or every day, if you command me."

So he went home, dug the earth in the corner pointed out to him, and there found the promised treasure.

I leave it to you to picture his joy, and that of his whole family.

Not wishing his neighbours to know that he had become so suddenly rich, he still continued to go to the wood, and gradually seemed to rise from poverty to wealth.

II.

At the end of the year, he went according to agreement to the forest. The voice cried, "So, you have come!" "Yes, Master," "And how have you fared?" "Well, Master, my family have good food and clothing, and we have reason to thank you every day." "You are well off, then, now; but tell me is there anything else you long for?" "Ah, yes, Master, I should like to be made Mayor of the village."

"All right, in forty days you shall be named Mayor."

"Oh, a thousand thanks, my clear protector, you are as good as newly-baked bread."

III.

The second year, the rich wood-cutter came to the forest in fine new clothes, and wearing, tied round his waist, the scarf of Mayor.

"Mr. Merlin," called he" come and speak to me."

"Here I am," said the voice, "what more do you wish?"

"Our Bishop died yesterday, and my son, with your aid, would like to replace him. A fresh favour, then, I ask of your kindness."

"In forty days, it shall be done," said Merlin.

IV.

Accordingly, in forty days, the son became a Bishop, and yet they were not contented.

At the end of the third year, the wood-cutter sought his protector, and in a low voice, called . "Merlin, will you do me another favour?"

"What is it?" said the voice.

"My daughter wishes to be the wife of a Director," said he. "So let it be," replied Merlin, "in forty clays, the marriage shall take place." And so it all came to pass.

V.

Then the wood-cutter spoke in this wise to his wife: "Why should I go again into the forest to speak to a creature whom I have never seen? I am wealthy enough now, I have plenty of friends, and my name is respected."

"Go once more," said she, "you ought to wish him good day, and thank him for all his benefits."

So the wood-cutter mounted his horse, and followed by two servants, entered the wood, and began to shout: "Merlot! Merlot! I have no more need of you, for I am sufficiently rich now." Merlin replied, "It seems that you have forgotten the time when you had not enough to eat, possessed only your hatchet, and could scarcely earn sixpence a day! The first service I rendered you, you went on your knees, and called me 'Master;' after the second, a little less polite, you said 'Mister;' after the third, only plain 'Merlin,' and now you have the impudence to address me as 'Merlot!' you think you have made your account well, and have no longer need of me. We'll see to that! You have always been heartless and stupid; continue to be stupid, and remain Poor as you were when I took you up." The rich man laughed, shrugged his shoulders, and did not believe a word that had been said to him.

He went back to his home. Soon his son, the Bishop died. His daughter, the Director's wife, also had a bad illness, and she died too. To crown his misfortunes, a war broke out, and the soldiers of each army entered his cellars, consumed his wine and his granaries of corn, and burned his maize in the field. His house also they set fire to, so he remained penniless, and uncared for.

VI.

When the time came for him to pay his taxes, he had no money in his purse, and was obliged to sell his farm. "See," said the ungrateful man, weeping, "I have lost all that I possessed—money, farm, house, children! Why did I not believe Merlin? It only remains for me to die, for I cannot bear this cursed life of a dog." "No, no," said his wife, "we must set to work again." "With what?" said he, "we have not even a donkey left!" "With what God gives us," said she.

God only gave them a basket, borrowed from a neighbour. With this on his back, and his hatchet in hand, he set off once more to the wood, to try to earn his sixpence a day.

Never more did he hear the voice of Merlin.

THE HERMIT'S FOUNDLING WITH
THE GOLDEN HAIR.

Once on a time there dwelt in a hollow of one of the great mountains a solitary Hermit, who had not seen the face of a human creature since he was a Child.

His only neighbours were the beasts of the forest, with whom he lived on very good terms.

One day when he had gone to fetch water from a neighbouring stream, he saw floating on its surface a tarred basket containing what seemed to be a bundle of clothes. To his astonishment the cries of a baby issued from this basket! Muttering a prayer, he plunged into the water, and with the aid of his staff drew the basket to the edge of the stream. In this basket was a boy of only a few weeks old. The Hermit took the little one in his arms, and its wailing ceased. On examining further he found attached to it a letter, saying that the infant was the unhappy son of a king's daughter, who for fear of her shame being brought to light, had sent her little one clown the stream to the care of the good God. The Hermit received the gift with joy, but when he thought of his own incompetence, and his inability to procure milk, or any suitable food for his little charge, he was in despair. Suddenly there began to grow near the entrance of his Cave, a Vine whose branches spread and climbed quickly up to the top of the Cave. It already bore grapes, of which some were ripe, others still green, others hardly formed, others in flower; taking of the ripe grapes, and squeezing the juice into the mouth of the little one, he saw that he sucked it in with relish.

So the child was fed on the juice of the grape until he had teeth to share the roots and other hard fare of his protector.

As he grow bigger, the Hermit taught him to read and write, to gather roots for their daily food, and to shoot birds with a bow and arrow.

The boy had now grown into a youth, when the Hermit called him, and thus said: My son, Dimitri (for thus had he baptized him), I find myself getting weaker every day, as you see I am very old, and I warn you that in three days from this, I shall go to another world. I am not your real father, for I rescued you from the stream when you had been abandoned in a basket by your mother, so as to hide the shame, and the punishment of her fault. When I sleep the last long sleep, which you will recognize by the coldness of my body, there will come a Lion; have no fear of him, he will make my grave, and you will cover me over with earth. I have no legacy for you except a horse's bridle. When I have left you for ever, then reach down from the top of the cave, the bridle, shake it, and a horse will appear at this summons, who will from henceforth be your guide."

On the third day after this, the Hermit was no more. On his hard couch he slept his long sleep. The Lion with his claws dug the grave, and Dimitri placed him gently therein and covered him over with earth, and wept three days and three nights for his benefactor.

On the third day, hunger reminded him that he had not eaten, so going to his vine for support, his astonishment was extreme on finding it withered, and with no grapes on it. Calling to mind the last instructions of the Hermit, he entered the cave, and found the bridle, on shaking which, appeared a Winged Horse, who enquired, "Master, what are your commands?" The youth recounted to him his past life, and how the Hermit had stood him in the stead of a parent.

"Let us go to some other country," said he, "for here with that grave before my eyes, I am always disposed to cry." Said the horse, "Just so, my Master, we will go and live where there are other men like you." "How," said Dimitri, "are there other men like me and my father? and shall we live amongst them?" "Certainly," answered the horse. Said the youth, "How is it that none of them have ever come here?"

"There is nothing to lead them to this mountain, we must go to them."

"Let us set off," said he, gleefully. "Yes," said the horse, "but you must be clothed; where we are going, they don't wear Lion and Tiger skins; put your hand in my right ear, and draw out what you will find." To Dimitri's surprise, there he found a suit of clothes, and aided by the instructions of the horse, he succeeded in putting them on. He mounted the horse, and submitted himself to its guidance.

On arriving at a City where men and women were moving about, as numerous as ants, our hero was dumb with astonishment and admiration at the houses, and at all which met his view.

Said the horse, "Master, here everyone has some trade, some occupation; you also must find something to do;" but the youth was unwilling, so after a few days sojourn, they set off again on their journey.

Soon they arrived at a Kingdom ruled over by three Fairies, and the horse advised Dimitri to try and enter their service.

With some difficulty he succeeded, and commenced his new duties. The horse visited him daily, and gave him instructions; he informed him that there was a room in the Fairies' Palace which contained a bath, and that once in a hundred years, the water in this bath had the power of changing into gold, the hair of the one who bathed first in it. Also that in a chest in the same room was a bundle of three suits of clothes, which they preserved with a jealous care. The Fairies had given the youth orders to clean all parts of the Palace, excepting the bath room, which he was strictly forbidden to enter. The Fairies being called away to a fairy festival, the youth all alone entered the forbidden chamber, and saw all as described by the horse, but the bath was without water. On the next absence of the fairies, before leaving, knowing that the time of the filling of the fountain was approaching, they instructed Demitri that if he heard the slightest noise in the bath room, to take a horn and sound it three times, so that they might return quickly.

Shortly after their departure, came the sound of rushing water from the bath room, the youth called at once for the horse who bade him enter the bath and bathe, then steal the bundle of clothes from the chest, then mount the winged horse and fly away.

When they had quitted. the palace, it began to shake and tremble to its foundations. This brought back the fairies, who seeing that the bath had been used and was no good for another hundred years, their bundle of precious clothes gone, and their servant absent, they set off in pursuit of the latter. They had nearly laid hands on him, when he passed the frontier of their power, and came to a sudden stop. At this disappointment the fairies could not restrain their anger but cried, "Son of an elf, how you have cheated us, lot us see at least your hair," he shook loose his hair and they continued, "who ever saw such hair? as bright as gold—only give us back the bundle of clothes and we will pardon you." "No!" said he, "I keep them instead of the wages you owe me," and then with his horse continued his journey.

Arrived in a town, he covered his hair with a close fitting bladder, and went to the gardener of the Governor of the town to seek service as under gardener.

As he was in need of a help, he engaged him to water the grass, weed the garden, and lop the trees.

This Governor was the father of three daughters, who were somewhat neglected and left to themselves, owing to their father's official duties. One day the eldest of the girls Anika, calling her sisters to her, said, "Let us each choose a melon to take to table for our father." This was done, the melons being served on golden plates. The Governor was so astonished that he summoned his council together and asked them to guess the meaning of this act of his daughters. They decided to cut open the melons, and found that one of them was beginning slightly to decay, that another was just ripe enough to eat, and that a third was only ripening.

Said the eldest councillor, "May your Excellence live many years! these melons are the ages of your daughters, and show the time is arrived for you to provide them with homes and with husbands." So the Governor decided that his daughters should be married, and even on the next day negotiations were entered into for their hands.

The eldest, Anika, soon made her choice, and after the marriage, the Governor accompanied his son-in-law and daughter to the frontier.

Only the youngest, Didine, remained at home.

Our hero, the under gardener, seeing that the *cortège* had set off, let down his hair, put on one of the fairy suits, called his horse and mounting it, danced all over the garden, crushing and destroying the flowers.

He was unaware that Didine was at the window watching all his movements. When he saw the folly he had committed, he changed quickly his dress, and began to repair the damage he had done. On his arrival, the head gardener was so vexed with the state of things, that he was on the point of giving our here a hearty thrashing. Didine, still looking on, tapped at the window and asked the gardener to send her some flowers. He made her up a bouquet, in return for which she sent him gold, and a request not to beat his under gardener.

Happy to have received such a handsome remuneration, the gardener with much trouble and pains made the garden in as good a state as it was before the folly of Dimitri. The marriage of the second daughter took place in a short space of time, and her father and his suite accompanied them also, to the frontier; Didine only remaining at home under the plea of indisposition. Dimitri repeated the same folly as on the marriage of the oldest sister, the only difference being that this time he wore the second suit belonging to the fairies. All was repeated as before, and to prevent his being beaten, Didine sent two handfuls of gold to the gardener in return for his flowers. Again he worked until the garden had once more got into good condition.

Shortly after this the Governor organised a great chase, and while hunting he narrowly escaped being torn to pieces by a wild boar; to celebrate his good fortune he raised a temporary kiosque in the wood, and bade all his friends come and make merry.

Didine only was not there, still on the plea of indisposition. Dimitri for the third time alone, recommenced his folly, and put on the third dress of the fairies which was embroidered with the sun on the chest, the moon on the back, and the morning and evening star on the sleeves.

This time he committed such havoc that it was impossible to re-arrange the garden.

The gardener's rage knew no bounds and he was on the point of giving Dimitri a beating when Didine tapped at the window and asked for flowers.

With difficulty were two or three flowers found which had escaped the hoofs of the horse, but she gave him three handfuls of gold and begged him not to lay hands on Dimitri. In five weeks the garden was restored and Dimitri made to promise that he would never more commit such mischief.

The Governor began to be anxious about his daughter Didine for she kept to the house and seemed always sad, he proposed that she should marry the son of a neighbouring Boyard but she would not entertain the idea, so he called his council and asked their advice. "Governor!" said they "you must build a great tower with a gateway, and all the pretenders to the hand of Didine must pass under it, give to her a golden apple which she must throw to the one whom she desires for her husband."

No sooner said than done, the tower was built, and it was soon spread abroad that all who wished to marry Didine must pass under this Archway. Many came, of both high and low degree, but still she did not throw the apple, and they began to believe that she had no wish to marry, until one of the councillors said, "Let all those who are in your court, all those who are employed on your estate, pass under also." So they were called, and last of all came Dimitri who with great difficulty was persuaded to pass under. Didine at once flung the apple at him. The Governor seeing this exclaimed, "it is a mistake, she has hit the wrong man, let all pass through again." This was done, and again Didine threw the apple to Dimitri. All agreed that there was no mistake this time, and so the father unwillingly consented to her choice.

They were married without any rejoicings and suffered to live in the Governor's court, Dimitri earning their living as a water carrier. They were laughed at by all, the servants even throw dust and sweepings in the direction of their room. Inside it was very different, the horse had brought there all the wonders of the world, not even in King's palaces were to be found such lovely things as in their wretched dwelling.

The other pretenders to the hand of Didine were so indignant at their rejection, that they united together to make war on the Governor. This caused him much pain, but he had no other alternative than to prepare for the struggle.

His two sons-in-law brought their retainers and Dimitri asked his wife to beg of the Governor to let him go to the battle. "Go from out of my sight," said the father, "you have broken my peace for ever." After much entreaty he was prevailed on to allow Dimitri to be there, if only as a water carrier for the soldiers.

So in a shabby working dress, astride a wretched horse, blind and lame, he set off in front. When the army caught him up, they found that his horse had sunk into a bog, and he was trying with all his might to extricate it. With laughs and jeers they passed on, leaving him alone to do the best he could. When they were out of sight, Dimitri swiftly donned the clothes of the fairies, and mounting his winged horse, sped to a commanding height, where he had a good view of the troops. Seeing that the enemy was eight times greater in number, he dashed into their midst, and slashing right and left, put them to rout in the greatest disorder. In the effort Dimitri cut his wrist, and the Governor gave him his handkerchief with which to bind it up.

When the Governor's army returned victorious, they again came upon Dimitri, still trying to extricate the miserable mare from the bog;

and being in good humour with their success, the Governor ordered his soldiers to come to his aid.

Shortly after this, the Governor fell ill and became totally blind. All the doctors, all the wise men, all the astrologers were called, but none could think of any remedy.

On awaking one morning, the Governor related that he had dreamt that if he washed his eyes with the milk of a wild red goat, he would regain his sight. Hearing this, his two sons-in-law set off in search of such a goat, without taking notice of Dimitri, or asking him to accompany them. He, on his side, went out alone, on his faithful steed, to the mountains where the red goats browsed.

Finding quickly both sheep and goats, Dimitri milked the sheep, disguised himself as a goat-herd, and was on the look out for his brothers-in-law. When they came up they asked him if he had milk to sell? He answered, yes, but that having heard of the Governor's dream, he was going to take this reel goat's milk to him. Enquiring if he would sell the milk to them, he said he would take no money for it, but that if they wished for the milk he would give them some, if they would allow him to mark them with his brand on their backs.

The sons-in-law taking council together, thought it would not do them much harm, so they consented to being branded, and taking the milk, set off quickly to the Governor. He took of the milk and drank it, he bathed his eyes with it, but it had no effect.

Some time after came Didine with a wooden pail, saying, "Father, take this milk and use it, it is brought by my husband-drink it, and bathe your eyes with it, I entreat you." The Governor answered, "What good has your stupid husband ever done to me? Is it likely he can be of any use now? Even your brothers-in-law who aided me in battle, are no good to me. Have I not forbade you my presence? How dare you intrude?" "I will submit to any punishment you may think fit, father, if you will but wash your eyes with this milk, which your loving daughter brings you." The Governor seeing that she was so importunate, bathed his eyes with the milk again and again, until he began to see dimly; continuing this, in a few days his sight was quite restored to him.

On the Governor's recovery he gave a great banquet, and Didine with her husband, Dimitri, were allowed to sit at the lower end of the table. While the festivity was at its height, Dimitri arose, and demanding pardon for the interruption, enquired of the Governor if it were right for slaves to sit at the same table as their masters. "Certainly not," said the Governor. "If that be the case, and as all the world knows you to be a just man, give me justice, and bid your right hand and your left hand guest, arise, for they are my slaves, for proof of which you will find them both branded with my mark."

When the sons-in-law heard this, they began to tremble, and were forced to confess the truth. They were bade to rise, and place themselves behind Dimitri's chair.

Later on Dimitri drew from his pocket, the handkerchief which the Governor gave him to bind his wrist after the battle. "How did you come by this handkerchief?" said the Governor, "for I gave it to the powerful man. sent from God to aid me in the battle." "Not at all," said Dimitri, "for you gave it to me." "Is it so? Could it have been you who stood us in such good stead."

"I alone," said Dimitri.

"It is impossible that I can believe this," said the Governor, "unless you stand before me precisely as you were when I gave you the handkerchief." Dimitri rose from the table, and going out quickly, returned clad in a suit of the fairies' clothes, and with his golden hair let down, to the astonishment of the Governor and his guests. All rose and saluted him on his entrance, the Governor complimented Didine on her choice, and feeling that he was growing old, said he wished to relinquish the Governorship in favour of Dimitri. This done, Dimitri's power and renown became world-wide talk. He pardoned his brothers-in-law, and gave them good posts in the country.

His winged horse returned to fairyland, bearing the three suits of charmed clothing, which he no longer needed. All that remained to him was his hair which was like threads of gold, from his having bathed in the magic bath.

His sons and daughters inherited his beautiful hair, and the old women to this day, believe that all true Dimitris ought to have hair as bright and golden as the ripe maize in their cornfields.

THE DAUGHTER OF THE ROSE.

IN clays gone by, there dwelt a King and a Queen in Jassy, who, to keep their only son at home with them, were always making him fine promises, which they never fulfilled.

One day this young Prince, Marin by name, went to his mother's apartments, and announced to her, that if she did not speedily bring to him the beautiful Princess from foreign parts which she had promised him to wife, he should set off in search of her himself. After waiting some weeks, finding that this promise was not likely to be fulfilled, he called for his horse and his retainers, and set off on his travels. He rode along until he came to a vast prairie, studded with the most beautiful flowers, through which meandered a silvery rivulet of pure water.

By the side of this rivulet grew a large rose tree with spreading branches, under which Marin stretched himself, and was trying to seek repose when he heard issuing from the tree these words:

> I pray thee sweet and loved rose tree,
> Open thy bark and let me free,
> To seek the brook's refreshing wave,
> To cool my face, my limbs to bathe,
> To cull sweet flowers to deck my brow,
> Then know'st my soul is pure as snow."

The rose tree unfolded, and from its centre came a fair golden-haired maiden, so dazzling, that to see her was brighter than sunlight. When the Prince Marin cast his eyes upon her, he was petrified at the sight of her beauty; but recovering his confidence he approached her and said, "lovely maiden, if you will give me a flower from your girdle, I will give you a nest in my palace; if you will give me a flower from your lips to kiss, I will dig up your rose tree and transplant it in the garden of my palace; if you will give me your love, I will make you Princess." The maiden, like most other young maidens, believed this flattery, and gave to Marin all that he asked and desired.

Sitting hand in hand talking of love, they fell asleep. Marin waking before the maiden, mounted his horse, and went on his way with his followers, leaving only a bunch of flowers in the lap of the sleeping girl. Journeying on, the young Prince arrived at length at a golden palace studded with topazes. He enquired of the first man whom he met, whether in that palace there dwelt a young Princess? It so happened that it was the owner of the palace to whom he had addressed himself, and who could boast of possessing a most charming daughter. He had heard of the good looks, and of the riches of this Prince of Jassy, and readily came to the conclusion that this could be no other but the young Marin, so he replied willingly, "Yes, here dwells the Princess Lexandra, and I am her father." Marin heard this with joy, and requested to be introduced into the Palace, with the view of soliciting the hand of the young Lexandra.

The invitation was given, and after some days' sojourn, and finding that the Princess was as lovely as she was good, and that he had found favour in her eyes, he set off with his future father-in-law, and intended bride, in a chariot to present her to his parents at Jassy.

* * * * *

The rose maiden on awaking, finding herself alone, and with but a bunch of flowers for her only companions, sighed and said, "dear little flowers, why have you made me sleep so long, and why have you separated me from my beloved?" Rising from the ground, she went up to the rose tree, and striking it, said:

> I pray thee, sweet and loved rose tree,
> Open thy bark, make place for me."

but the rose tree would not unfold itself, and only answered, "Go away, my pretty maiden, for you have sinned and can no more enter here."

Weeping, she turned aside, and seeing that she could no more be received in the bosom of the rose tree, seizing a staff she set off on the same road as that which the young Marin had taken. After going some distance she met with a Monk, and entreated him to exchange with her his rough frock and cowl, in return for her rich dress. He accepted willingly; the maiden wrapped herself in his garment and went on her way. On the confines of a wood, being very weary, she seated herself under the shade of a large elm, in order to take a little rest; shortly after, she saw in the distance a chariot drawn by eight horses approaching, and as it drew near, she recognised her faithless lover.

"Good day, young Monk," said Marin. "I thank thee, Highness," said the Monk, approaching the carriage. "From whence come you?" said Marin. "From the valley," said the Monk. "What did you see there?" asked the Prince. "Nothing, very extraordinary," said the Monk, "only near to a large rose tree, there was a beautiful girl weeping, and on my enquiring the cause of her grief, she told me her history." "Repeat it to us," said Marin, visibly moved. "This was what she told me," said the Monk, "that her home had been in a rose tree, where she was loved and nurtured; that coming out one day in search of flowers, she met with a young Prince, who begged a flower from her waist, which she gave him." Now the Monk looked fixedly at the Prince, but the latter bade him go on with the story. "Then he asked a flower from her mouth to kiss, and then for her love, and she gave even that also." "Go on," said the Prince. "Sitting hand in hand amongst the flowers, sleep overtook them; but when the maiden awoke she found herself deserted, and only a bunch of flowers on her lap. Going to the rose tree, she repeated the rhyme which would open its bark to admit her into its body; but the rose tree remained solid and firm, because she was no longer worthy to enter within, and for this the young girl was weeping alone, and in misery." "Is that all?" said the Prince. "So far as I know, for I left her crying in the field." "To what town are you going, my good Monk?" asked the Prince. "To the same as your Highness, to Jassy," said he. "Jump into our carriage, then," said the Prince, opening the door and making place for him. The Monk accepted readily, and during the whole of their journey, the Prince questioned him for further news of the young maiden.

Arrived in the Capital, and at the home of Marin, he invited the Monk to be his guest, and gave him a room next to his own in the palace. Yet in three days this marriage with the Princess Lexandra was to take place, and still Marin could not forget the rose maiden, and each evening on passing the door of the Monk, he would stay to talk about her.

At length the wedding day approached, and the Monk disappeared.

One evening, the Prince stopped as usual at the Monk's door, hoping to hear more of the deserted maiden; but for answer he only heard a muffled sigh! Breaking open the door, he saw the poor Monk suspended by a cord to a large book on the wall; cutting him down, and taking off the Monk's frock, underneath it the golden hair and the pale face of the rose maiden met his view. Then he called the King and Queen-his parents, and exclaimed, "Look! this is *my* Princess, do what you will with the other."

So the Princess Lexandra was sent back home with her father, and with great riches, enough for her dower, and the rose maiden was married to the Prince Marin, and they had many children and lived very happily ever after.

THE TWELVE-HEADED GRIFFIN.

ONCE upon a time there lived a King and Queen whose greatest blessing from God was an only child of fifteen, named Theodor.

This boy from his childhood had learnt to ride, and to shoot with the bow, and had become a great proficient in both arts.

One day while practising archery, one of his arrows shot out of sight. The boy having marked the direction which it took, went to his father to request his swiftest horse, and money to go in search of his arrow.

His father gave him money, and permission to take the best horse in his stables.

With joy the boy mounted swiftly, and set off at a gallop.

After riding long and far, so far that the sun was disappearing from the horizon, he found himself in a vast prairie full of flowers. Stopping his horse, standing up in his stirrups, and shading his eyes with his hand, he perceived his arrow sticking in the ground. Dismounting he went quickly to the spot, seized the arrow with both hands, and with difficulty drew it out, leaving a great hole in the earth where it had penetrated. On looking down this hole, he saw at the bottom of it, a fine bull, and on the bull's back, a sword and a letter.

In great surprise at all these strange surroundings, he opened the letter and read, "Whomsoever will take this bull and will give it three pecks of wheat and a gallon of wine, and continue to do so daily, the bull will have power to bring back to life the man who does this, no matter how many times he may die. This sword will turn into stone any living or inanimate object."

Leading the bull, and strapping on the sword, the boy went on his way.

Towards night he reached a city and asked food and shelter of an old woman whom he met with. For himself a draught of water, for the bull a gallon of wine. The old woman fed him and his animals, and gave the requisite wine to the bull. *Water* she said she had none, for in the whole city there was but one fountain, and that at the outskirts of the town; and that this fountain was guarded by a twelve-headed monster. Whomsoever needed water must sacrifice a young maiden to his appetite.

She told him that the next day it was the King's turn to give his daughter, and that this said King had made a proclamation to the effect, that whosoever would kill this monster and save his daughter, immense riches, and the hand of his daughter in marriage would be the reward.

The youth hearing all this, requested the old woman to awake him very early next morning, and to give him her water-jars, saying he would fill them without giving anything to the monster. She promised this, and he soon fell into a sound sleep.

According to promise the next morning she aroused him, and taking his sword, his bow and arrows, and the water-jars, set off for the well. Arrived there, he found the King's daughter weeping, and waiting to be eaten by the monster. Said the youth to her, "I have come to deliver you from the fangs of the monster, on one condition, that is, that you let me sit down by your side, lay my head on your lap, and if I should fall asleep, not to awake me until the monster shews himself."

The young girl acquiesced with joy, and sitting clown beside her, the youth laid his head on her lap, and soon fell asleep. When the monster made his appearance, the girl was so overwhelmed with terror that she could not awake the youth, but cried so plentifully that the scalding tears fell on his face. Jumping up, he saw the Monster before him. Charging his bow, he placed himself in front of the maiden; the monster seeing this, exclaimed, "Stand aside, and let me take my right," but the youth refused, it the same time drew the string of his bow and sent an arrow into the head which was stretched forth for his destruction.

The monster writhed with pain, and projected a *second* head, and then began a terrible strife. The youth's only defence was his courage and his bow, but the monster had his twelve heads, and his poisoned breath.

All that long summer's day they fought until evening; as night fell the boy could hardly stand from fatigue, had broken his bow, and had but one arrow in his quiver. But, on the other hand, the monster remained with only one head left out of the twelve.

At length, the youth took from the maiden's head, a long mesh of her rich hair—she, more dead than alive from terror, and with it bound his broken bow together, and the fight recommenced. Eventually the youth was victorious, but fell down faint from loss of blood.

While both these young creatures lay fainting by the well side, there came up a Tzigan, in the service of the King, to fetch water. Seeing the monster annihilated, he sought the young Princess, and finding that she was not dead, but only in a swoon, he threw water over her, and she quickly returned to her senses. The Tzigan enquired of her who had killed the monster, and the maiden pointed to the apparently dead Theodor. Quick as thought the Tzigan seized the youth's sword, and cut his body into hundreds of pieces.

Then, collecting the twelve heads and tongues of the monster, and charging the maiden not to tell to the King who had performed this mighty deed, he accompanied her to her father's palace.

Without the knowledge of the Tzigan, the maid let fall a ring, and a handkerchief, beside the remains of the slaughtered youth.

When the King saw his daughter approach, he was overwhelmed with joy, and demanded the name of her deliverer. "I, mighty King," replied the Tzigan, with pride. "Can this be true?" enquired the King. "It is true," said his daughter, tremulously.

Though the King was sorely grieved that the deliverer of his child was a gipsy, and a slave, yet he felt bound to fulfil the promise that she should be given him to wife.

II.

While Theodor was lying hewed in morsels, by the side of the well, the old woman, his hostess, went to her stable to feed and give drink to the Bull. On seeing her, he refused all nourishment, telling her that "he was thirsting after water, and not after wine, and that she must lead him to the public well; as now that the monster existed no longer, all the world could drink water in peace." He bade her take with them a lump of salt, and soon they arrived at the well.

When the woman saw the morsels of what had once been the brave youth, she began to cry aloud; but the bull said to her, "Don't distress yourself in that way, but do as I tell you: take up piece by piece, limb by limb, and place them together, as they were in life." Obeying him, she put the different members once more together again. The bull licked well the lump of salt, then breathed over, and licked the youth. Wherever his tongue passed over, the marks of the sword disappeared, and when he once more breathed into his face, Theodor opened his eyes and exclaimed: "Have I slept long?" "You would have slept longer," said the woman, "if your bull had not brought you to life."

All was as a dream to him, and it was only after the bull had explained all that had occurred, that he understood why the maiden was no longer by his side.

On looking around him he saw the ring and the handkerchief which she had dropped; he took possession of them, and they returned to the old woman's dwelling.

The following day the King caused a proclamation to be issued to the effect that the nuptials of his beloved daughter, with Burcea, the Tzigan, would take place in eight days. Burcea her deliverer, inviting the neighbouring Kings and Nobles to come and do honour to the ceremony.

He sent for the court tailor, and commanded for his future son-in-law, clothing befitting his new rank. He ordered his treasurer to pay to Burcea, any sum of money which he might demand.

On the appointed day, the guests were assembled in the Imperial Palace; but all were melancholy, and angry, that an ugly, uneducated gipsy, should have gained such a high-born, lovely bride.

Amongst them all, the King was the most grieved, with the exception, perhaps, of his daughter, who reproached herself for not having told the truth to the King, her father.

Burcea, the Tzigan, alone, was joyful.

In those days, it was the custom at the marriage of a King's daughter, for each subject to offer a present, according to his means; so Theodor begged the old woman to make him a cake, which she should take to the palace as his offering. She willingly agreed, and began to make the cake. When it was ready for the oven, the youth slipped the ring into the middle of the cake, and covered the paste over it.

The cake was baked, and wrapped in a clean napkin, and taken by the old woman to the gate of the palace. Her dress was so old and so patched, that the servants forbade her to enter; but the Princess looking from the window, gave orders that she should be admitted, and brought into her presence.

This was quickly done, and the cake was offered with humble wishes for her future happiness. The Princess took the cake and broke it; imagine her surprise when she found her ring in the middle of it! "Where is the person who put this ring here?" asked she of the old woman. "It must be the handsome boy that is at my cottage," said she, "he who was hewn to pieces by your slave, and was restored to life and health by his friendly bull."

"Take this purse of money for yourself," said the Princess," and return quickly to your home, tell my deliverer to come here, for I am awaiting him."

The woman sped swiftly on her errand. Full of joy, the youth seized his sword, and taking the handkerchief, set off for the Imperial palace.

On reaching the reception ball, he saw a crowd of Nobles, and in their centre, Burcea the Tzigan, swelling with pride, and thinking himself as powerful as a Grand Vizier.

The youth passed speedily on, until he reached an apartment where the Princess was reclining. Seeing him, she sprang up, and flung herself into his arms, crying out, "this is my deliverer, this is my deliverer."

A crowd quickly surrounded them, and Theodor, in a clear voice, said: "It is true that I am the deliverer of this maiden, who would have been eaten by the monster of the well. I killed him, and she was free; but faint from fatigue and loss of blood, when a slave of the King's, coming to the well, and seeing me in this state, hewed me to pieces with my own sword, and threatened the maiden with death, if she avowed the truth. At the same time he possessed himself with the proofs of the monster's destruction. Had it not been for a bull, endowed with a miraculous power of bringing the dead to life, I should now be ready for my grave. Seeing that many wise men are here, and knowing that there is wisdom in numbers, I entreat all present to judge and condemn the one who is guilty."

"To death! to death!" cried the crowd.

The Emperor, calling his servants, ordered them to bring two horses from his stables, one bred in the mountains, the other bred in the plains, and to tie the limbs of Burcea, the Tzigan, to these two animals; his order was obeyed, the horses were let loose, and setting off in a galop in different directions, the body of the slave was torn limb from limb.

And now, indeed, there was a real rejoicing; but the marriage, and the court festivities were all postponed, until the arrival of the parents of

Theodor, who embraced him, and wept for joy and pride, that he had so nobly distinguished himself.

They built for him, and his young bride, a magnificent palace; at the entrance to the court-yard, there was also a well of purest water, apparently guarded and watched over by a gigantic bull in marble.

VASILICA THE BRAVE.

ONCE upon a time, in a certain town there dwelt a gipsy blacksmith, who was the best iron worker in the whole empire.

This gipsy had a son as fair and handsome as a Roumanian fawn, and as strong and as brave as a young lion. He played with the sledge hammer as if it were a toy; twisted the great anvil between his fingers, and broke across his knee a thick iron bar as though it were a reed.

The life of a working blacksmith, however, was not to his taste, athletic sports, and playing at soldiers with his young comrades pleased him better, pretending that he was a great Captain, and strutting about in a coloured paper helmet. He liked racing and wrestling, and running about in the open air all day long,—to quarrel, and to come off victorious. As I have already said, he was very strong, stronger than the strongest man. He did not know the meaning of fear, and was calm and cool in the greatest peril; he laughed at ill the frightful tales of dragons and evil spirits recounted by the old women of the neighbourhood.

So he was called Vasilica the Brave.

His father, seeing that he was not diligent at learning, either his own trade, or any other, thought it best that he should become a soldier. But the boy did not wish to be placed under the command of others, for with his strength he could overcome them all.

Seeing that his father was always urging him to take to some business, and now that he was grown to manhood, the time had arrived for him to gain his livelihood, he made a small bundle of his clothes, and left home without telling anyone where he was going to, or without having come to any conclusion himself on that point.

II.

As he went along the highway, his bundle on a stick slung over his shoulder, he heard in the distance the neighing and shrieking of a horse, enough to make his hair stand on end.

Another in his place would have turned back; he, on the contrary, threw his bundle on the grass, and ran quickly in the direction from whence the sound came, and before he could say "God help me," he reached a large field in the middle of which a terrible scene met his view. A large and awful dragon was twisting itself round a beautiful horse, squeezing the very life out of its body, beating it with its wings, and biting it with its ferocious mouth, until the poor animal was covered with blood.

The horse, though strong and brave, had only his teeth and hoofs to defend himself with, so that the dragon, having so great an advantage, would soon have finished the strife.

When the horse saw Vasilica appear, he called to him, "quick! quick! come here and save me, I shall be of much use to you in the world."

Then the dragon, said, "mind your own affairs, youngster, if you do not wish to be ground to powder."

Vasilica had no weapon, but hearing the dragon calling to him with so much assurance, fearlessly rushed towards him, careless of his tail, which beat the ground like a thousand whips, seized him by the head from behind, jerked it once upwards, twisted it to the right and to the left, and the dragon's head remained in his hands. The wings of the terrible animal became as powerless as those of a wet turkey, its tail no longer beat the ground, and its body fell in a heap below.

The horse, freed from the terrible grip, shook

FIGHT OF HORSE AND DRAGON.

himself, throwing the foam in all directions, and going up to Vasilica said, "master, I thank thee; be thou my master until death."

III.

Now we find Vasilica with the horse, and such a horse! After having caught his bundle, he mounted quickly, and scratched his ear in hesitation, not knowing what direction to take.

"Where are we going, master?" said the horse, seeing his indecision.

"I scarcely know!" said Vasilica, looking in various directions.

"Where are you going?" again said the horse.

"Where I shall be able to do brave deeds, don't you know that I am the renowned Vasilica?" said he with pride.

"Vasilica the brave! Oh, I have heard mention of this name with fear, and if what you say is true, go where I will take you, and you will find what you seek."

"What sayest thou?"

"I say that if thou art really the renowned Vasilica, then thou must do a brave and good deed, that is, to rescue my mistress and her three sisters from three fearful dragons, that have held them in their power for so many years."

"Are these dragons formidable?" asked Vasilica, "Indeed, yes," replied the horse, "no man has yet dared to approach one of them in strength or in power."

"Let me only encounter them; I have a lance in readiness for them," said Vasilica.

"Don't boast, master, for you do not know with whom you have to do, my first master was not to be despised, but nevertheless, he was eaten alive by the weakest of these dragons; had the other taken him in hand, who is the strongest in the world, then what would have become of him?"

"Who was your master?" asked Vasilica.

"He was the son of a powerful emperor, who fell in love with the daughter of a neighbouring emperor, and when he went to ask her in marriage, the father replied, 'first of all you must rescue the two other sisters from the power of the dragons, and when you have done this, I will give you my daughter to wife.' My master joyfully agreed to this proposal, and made his preparations to depart. But during the night, the dragons came and carried off also his intended bride, which only increased his eagerness to depart. The emperor's son was brave, but imprudent, and lily advice was useless, for he would not listen to me, and so in consequence fell all easy prey to those monsters, who took his life without the slightest remorse. Since then I have been without a master, wandering about, searching for some brave personage of renown, to revenge the death of my master, and to rescue those three unhappy

Princesses from life-long captivity. Many years have passed since I began my search, and I have been unable to find any one who dared to put his strength in opposition to that of the dragons. To-day, passing by here, I encountered the hideous monster, who nearly cut the thread of my life, and would have done so had it not been for your valiant and powerful arm."

"Pray tell me, where do these dragons live?" said Vasilica.

"You must traverse nine kingdoms, and cross nine seas; but have no anxiety on that account, for I am a flying horse, and can go like the wind, and gallop as quick as thought. I can transform myself to any shape I please, and have also the same power over others; come with me, rescue these unfortunate sisters from captivity, I am sure you will vanquish these terrible dragons, and become possessed of their boundless treasures, for I have heard them often say, '*if ever Vasilica the brave crosses our path, our power is at an end.*'"

"Let us go," said Vasilica, with pride; the horse spread his wings, and they disappeared from sight.

IV.

AFTER having gone some distance through the clouds, the horse and rider descended in a green field, studded with numberless flowers, in the centre of which stood a castle, all in copper, and which glistened quite dazzling in the sun.

"This is the palace of the biggest dragon," said the horse "go, knock at the gate, and it will be opened by the eldest Princess. Enter without fear, for the dragon is absent, and when he returns, you will know of it, for he will fling his club six miles before him, which club will enter the castle alone, and hang itself up on its own nail in the wall. If you wish to acquaint him with your presence, take up the club, fling it back, and go forwards and meet him."

Vasilica listened attentively, dismounted by the side of the wall, left the horse there to feed, and went straight to the Gate of the Palace, where he knocked three times.

The eldest Princess was walking alone in the court of the palace without attendants, and when she heard the knocking at the gate, she opened it in person.

Since she had been spirited away by the dragon, her eyes had not rested on a human creature, for the palace was situated in an uninhabited country.

Seeing Vasilica, she uttered a cry of surprise, and stood like a statue.

"Good day, Princess!" said Vasilica.

"Thank you! brave knight," stammered she.

"What wind has blown you here?"

"A favourable wind," said he, "the wind of freedom."

"May God hear you! but I cannot believe it," said she, with a sigh.

"Will you allow me, lady, a little rest and shelter?" asked Vasilica, entering the court.

"With very good will," said she, "only you must enter quickly, or the dragon will find you here."

Leave that to me, lady, I am a match for him."

So she sheltered her guest, and offered him all that she had of the best, according to the old Roumanian traditions of hospitality, without asking who he was, from whence he came, or whither he was going.

After he seemed refreshed, she began to question him of the world in general. While Vasilica was recounting to her what had happened lately, they suddenly heard a tremendous bellowing, followed by a trembling of the ground which shook the castle to its foundations. On hearing this, the Princess became pale as death, and cried, "Woe is me! Where shall I hide you—for the dragon is coming?" "Have no anxiety on my account, for we are safe," answered Vasilica. At that same moment, the gate was flung open, and the dragon's club was thrown in; with a whistling noise it sprung on to a table, and from thence hung itself on a nail.

Vasilica seeing this, seized the club from the nail, and turning it round in a circle three times, flung it beyond the gate twice the distance which it had originally come. The dragon coming along at a rapid pace towards the palace, hearing the roar of his club, stopped and exclaimed to himself, "What can this mean?" Hardly had he finished this exclamation, before his club clove through the air and fell at his feet, and penetrated the earth for a yard deep.

"My club!" cried the dragon, unearthing his weapon with great difficulty. "Who has dared to lay hands on this, and to throw it with all its weight, such a tremendous distance? Only Vasilica the Brave is capable of such an act."

"You have guessed well, monster," answered a voice close by, "Vasilica stands before you! I bow with humility in your presence."

"Ha! it is you," cried the dragon, grinding his teeth; "it is well you have come, for how long have I not thirsted for your blood? Tell me quickly what method of combat do you prefer? Wrestling, or the sword thrust?" "Wrestling is better, because it is more equal," said Vasilica. "Good, so be it," cried the dragon, dashing towards him so as to crush him with the weight of his body; but he had found his match at last though his size was gigantic, while Vasilica appeared slight, but sinewy and well knit. When he closed with the dragon, and flung his arms round him, it was with a grip of iron, and his muscles stood out like the tendons of a bull. The dragon flung himself to the right, but Vasilica twisting to the left nearly overthrow him.

The first struggle did not prove victorious to either, for they were both strong and brave.

They fought hand to hand, three hours, without relaxation; their feet had entered the ground up to their knees; perspiration was pouring from them, as from a fountain; the blood was trickling from their wounds, but neither would yield. Towards sunset, Vasilica concentrated all his force, and with one mighty push overthrew the dragon, thrust his dagger into his throat, and, finally, beheaded him, flinging the body into the moat. Dragging the head along with him to the palace, at the feet of the Emperor's daughter, he cried, "Princess, behold! Thou art a widow; but thou art free from the demon who kept thee enslaved."

"May God repay you tenfold," replied the Princess, weeping for joy.

V.

Finding herself delivered from the dragon, sunshine returned to the face of the Princess, and she set before her deliverer the best food she had; and entertained him for a week to restore himself, and recruit his strength.

At the end of this time, our hero took leave of the Princess, and mounting his horse flew off into the air. On descending, he saw glittering in the rays of the sun, a palace in pure silver.

"Here," says the horse, "is the residence of the second dragon, and he is more powerful than the one whose head you cut off; and yet he is less formidable than the third dragon. Go to his palace without fear, acquit yourself as you did with the first."

Vasilica departed, and knocking at the gate, it was opened by the second Princess, who remained equally astonished as her eldest sister had been. She received him with joy, and entertained him hospitably. While at the table the club of the second dragon entered, jumped from the table to the hook in the wall; the performance being accompanied by even a louder noise than on the previous occasion.

The Princess became pale, and trembled with fright; but Vasilica, with the greatest coolness, took the club from its resting place, and sent it back with two-fold force.

He set off at once to meet the dragon, who, seeing his club whirling through the air, and burying itself at his feet, in the ground, for a depth of two feet, in his turn became pale and said: "Only Vasilica the Brave, can have done this, and if he has reached so far as here, then surely my eldest brother is dead."

"You are correct in your calculations," said Vasilica, appearing on the scene, "be quick and prepare yourself for battle, I am thirsting to drink your blood, as I drank that of your brother."

"Don't be too sure about that," cried the dragon furiously, "shall we wrestle or fight with swords?"

"Wrestling is more equal," said Vasilica.

They fought for four long hours, and strove one against the other with so much force, that they sank into the ground up to their waists. Rivers of perspiration ran from them, but neither one nor the other would yield.

Towards night-fall, Vasilica, by a superhuman effort, gave the dragon a grip, and throw him heavily down, he made great efforts to rise, but the well-tempered dagger of Vasilica, entered his throat in an instant, and his life-blood welled out and stained the whole field.

Seeing that the dragon did not move, Vasilica cut off his head, and hid the trunk under a bridge.

On entering the palace he was received with great joy by the Princess, and remained her guest for two weeks.

VI.

AFTER taking leave of the Princess, Vasilica again mounted his horse, and they flew away into space. On descending towards the earth a third time, a shining golden palace met their view. When they were near it, the horse said to its master, "up to this time we have done our best, and we have come out victorious; but now you must be very cautious, for this is the most terrible of all the dragons, and the strongest creature that ever lived."

"So far I have told you to go forward and conquer, but now I say, reflect, while there is yet time."

"Vasilica does not fly from danger," answered he with pride; "if I turn back, the youngest Princess, who was the intended bride of your first master, and for whom he sacrificed his life, will remain in captivity; how then can you tell me to flee?"

"Do as you like!" said the horse, "only I repeat, reflect! and be careful; I also will try and help you, put faith in me, and with God's blessing, we will be victorious." With this conversation, they arrived in front of the palace, Vasilica dismounted, knocked at the gate, and entered as he had previously done, being received by the youngest daughter of the Emperor.

When at table, the third dragon announced himself by his club; Vasilica seized it, before it had time to place itself on the nail, and threw it out twice as quickly as it came in.

The dragon was approaching the bridge when he saw his club pelting along, and burying itself in the ground at his feet.

"This is the work of Vasilica the Brave," cried the dragon, foaming at the mouth; "he has killed my two brothers, and now I intend to kill him."

"Get to work, then," said Vasilica, obstructing his path.

"Well!" cried the dragon, how shall we fight? by wrestling, or by the sword?"

"Wrestling, as with the others," said Vasilica.

They closed at once, and now it was a fearful trial of strength, and they fought from noon to eventide. They had kicked up the earth until it reached their throats; Perspiration poured from them like a foaming cascade; blood spurted from their veins like water from a pump, and yet neither was victorious.

Fighting in this way, the dragon suddenly jumped from the hole in which he found himself, on to the bridge, and changed himself into a flaming red dragon, with a mouth quite two yards wide, and a seven forked tail. Hardly had this taken place, than Vasilica, by the aid of his horse, took the form of a green dragon, just as formidable as his adversary.

Dashing at each other with open mouths and tails erect, they met in the centre of the bridge, and they began to bite each other, to beat with their wings, and to lash with their tails. This unparallelled combat lasted till midnight: from their bodies oozed streams of black blood, from their eyes shot sparks of fire, from their nostrils sulphur, and from their mouths tongues of flame.

The red dragon became only a wheel of fire, and rolled quickly into the green dragon, so as to cut him in twain.

At the same moment, the green dragon was also a green wheel of flaming fire, and beat into the red wheel with unheard of force.

After this strife had lasted more than two hours, the red wheel demanded respite, seeing that its axle from the rapid motion, had taken fire; but the green wheel would not consent, although sparks of fare were perceptible in its axle also. At this moment, high up in the air above their heads, appeared a vulture.

"Vulture, dear vulture," cried the red wheel, "go down to the river, dip your wings in water, and come and wet my axle, then I will give you a dead body to feed on."

"Vulture, dear vulture," cried the green wheel, "go down to the river, dip your wings in water, and come and wet my axle, and then I will give you three dead bodies to feed on."

The vulture went to the river, clipped his wings, and wetted the axle of the green wheel. Instantaneously its force was redoubled, and it attacked its enemy with renewed power.

The red wheel was one sheet of livid fire, and exploded with a deafening noise.

The green wheel became once more Vasilica, who, dagger in hand, struck the red wheel, which also took its original shape, poured out streams of blood, and fell lifeless.

Vasilica, seeing the monster stretched on the bridge stiff and dead, out off its head, and kicking the carcase towards the vulture, cried, "there, eat this, and afterwards the other two dragons, which I have left near the drawbridges of their palaces." "I do not need them," answered the vulture, who speedily changed himself into the faithful horse.

"How is this?" cried Vasilica. "You, my deliverer?" as he saw his beloved horse by his side. "Yes, Master," said the horse, "I have kept my promise; I changed you into a dragon, and into a wheel of fire, when you needed it, and I have given you all the help in my power."

"You have repaid your debt," said Vasilica, "for you have saved my life, and now we are quits. Let us go and set. at liberty the youngest Princess, and then we will return home."

"He! he! we haven't yet time to go back."

"Why?" asked Vasilica. "We have yet more to do," said the horse; "we have conquered the dragons, but their mother yet remains, and she is more formidable than they."

"Come along," said Vasilica, impetuously, "let us go and vanquish her also."

"Not so fast, my master, we must rest awhile, for we have striven hard, and we have yet much to do."

"Lot us go to the Palace, then," said Vasilica.

The youngest princess, on learning that she was free from captivity, clapped her hands with joy, and entertained her deliverer and his valiant horse for three weeks, with the best that the castle afforded.

VII.

After three weeks had elapsed, the horse called his master aside one day, and said to him: "Master, we have had great trouble before we got free from those three monsters, and as yet we have not gained much; for the Princesses for whom we have fought, are even yet in great danger, until we have overcome the artful mother of the dragons."

"Let us set off at once," said Vasilica, vaulting into the saddle.

"It is easy to say 'Go,' but it is rather difficult to attain, for this she-dragon cannot be fought by wrestling, or by the sword, but must be combatted with her own weapons of cunning and deceit; and she is as deceitful as she is wicked. She will meet you with a kiss, and stab you from behind. If we can entrap her youngest daughter, we may then well say that we have got the upper hand. She has three daughters, all very lovely, but the youngest is perfection. If by fair means or foul, we can entice this young creature away, then the old one is in our power."

"If it be only a question of turning the head of a pretty girl, leave me alone for that, for I am a proficient in the art," said Vasilica, swelling with pride.

"He! he! master," it is not all plain sailing; the girl, perhaps, you maybe able to charm; but the old one has a keen scent, and directly she smells who you are, it is finished with us."

"Come along, and we'll see what happens."

They flew along, over vale, mountain, and forest, until a golden palace, put together with large diamond nails, came in sight. The dragoness had not yet received news of the death of her three sons; had she done so, the earth would have quaked at their approach.

In the beautiful garden, at the back of the palace, she was taking the air with her daughters, when her youngest daughter heard, near to her, the purring of a cat; on looking down, there was a beautiful little white kitten at her feet, playing and rubbing itself against the bottom of her robe.

"Ah! mother," said she, "see what a pretty kitten;" at the same time taking it up in her hands. Her mother not hearing her, she kept the kitten in her arms, entered a *kiosque* near, and seating herself on a low divan, took it on her lap and began patting and caressing it. The kitten rolled on its back, purring, and tapping her hands with its soft paws, and while playing, her kerchief slipped off her neck.

All at once the mother enters, and sniffing to the right and to the left, exclaimed: "There's the smell of man's flesh here, from the other world!"

"A man," said the girl, astonished, "what do you mean?" and went on playing with the kitten.

"There is no one here, I assure you."

"No one has come? You are stupid my child, it is a pity that you are my daughter. Throw a handkerchief round your neck, for it is not decent to sit there without one."

"But where do you see even the shadow of a man, mother?"

"Where? What is that on your lap?"

"Don't you see? It is a kitten."

"Kitten, kitten," said the mother, "but his eyes sparkle like those of a brave man; put on your kerchief, and you, kitten, take back your own shape, and come to table, for my house is open to all well meaning travellers. If you don't obey me, I will tear you in a thousand pieces."

The kitten, to whom this was addressed, went on with his play, taking no more notice than an actual kitten would.

This indifference, enraged the dragoness.

"Youngster!" she exclaimed, "if you don't take your original shape, I will fling you into the pond in the garden, which is very deep, and as cold as ice."

Still the kitten remained impassive, so she seized it by the nape of the neck, and carried it to the edge of the pond, again repeating her command. The kitten for reply began to play with a morsel of ribbon hanging from her dress.

"Let him alone, mother! Don't fling him into the pond! Don't you see it is a kitten, like all kittens? If he had been a man, he would have been afraid, and would have obeyed you."

"Don't speak! for you don't know what you say," said the dragoness, and seizing the kitten, she was about to throw it into the water.

The girl cried entreatingly that her kitten might not be drowned; the kitten, seeing its peril, stuck its claws into the dragoness, and scratched her so severely, that she flung it away from her in disgust.

"You are rightly punished," said her daughter, "now are you convinced that it is a kitten?"

"Kitten! kitten! but his eyes are man's eyes," cried the mother, in uncontrollable rage.

"Be so good as to let my kitten alone, for it is the only plaything I have ever had," said the girl, going after it, and holding it to her bosom.

But the dragoness was not easily deceived, and seizing her daughter by the hand, dragged her indoors, entered the kitchen, opened the door of the oven, and taking the kitten from her daughter said, "now sir, if you won't change yourself into a man, I will throw you into the hot oven."

The kitten's only reply was to play with a lighted ember, and burning itself, began to mew with pain, and jumped through the window.

The girl pursued it, hoping to catch and caress it, but the kitten was already over the wall and on the road beyond; the young girl hurried through the gate to catch it, so that it might not escape into the wood.

She was too late, for it was already in the wood, and forgetting the danger incurred, she set off in pursuit.

The kitten enticed the maiden slowly along, but as soon as she tried to catch it, it slipped through her fingers, and glided gently forwards, so that before she was aware of it, she found herself in the middle of a dense forest.

Then the kitten suddenly transformed himself into Vasilica the Brave, seized the maiden in his arms, sprang with her on to his faithful horse, and journeyed many hours, until he reached his native city.

Who can recount the rejoicings of his parents, the joy of his comrades, the happiness, and the wealth of the young couple? Vasilica, in every palace which he visited, had received gifts of precious stones, so that his leather girdle was as full of diamonds and sapphires, as is his native country now of his valiant descendants.

"HANDSOME IS AS HANDSOME DOES."

ONCE on a time, there lived an old man and an old woman; each had two children by previous marriages. The wife took good care of her own children, feeding them well, and giving them good clothes; while the children, of the husband were neglected, and left almost without food. Not content with thus ill-treating them, and seeing that they were better looking, and better behaved, than her own, she made up her mind to get rid of them.

So one day she said to her husband, "your boy and girl are too lazy and good-for-nothing, you must send them from here, or I will not eat bread and salt out of the same platter with you again.

"Where can I take them to?" asked he.

"Where you please, so long as I am no longer troubled with them."

Finding no other way of pacifying his wife, he determined to take them next day to a wood and leave them there. The boy overheard the conversation, and repeated it to his sister; so they took their precautions, and next morning they each filled a canvas bag, one with ashes, the other with *malain* (corn flour), before their father called them to accompany him, and on the way, the boy scattered the ashes. On arriving at the four cross roads, the father bade them wait there for him, as he was going further into the forest to cut down some branches.

Giving them some food, he disappeared amongst the thickets, and tying a hollow gourd to a tree, he returned by another way to his cottage.

When the wind blew, it struck the gourd against the tree, and produced a sound like wood-chopping, so when the children heard this they said, "hark, to father, cutting wood!"

Waiting half the day, and seeing that their father did not come, they set off to search him from whence the sound came. On reaching the tree from whence the noise proceeded they found only the gourd; so they began to cry, but by the aid of the traces of the ashes, found their home again.

The parents, with the wife's children were sitting round the fire eating long white loaves, the outside of which being burnt, the wife said to her husband it where are your children that they may cat these spoiled pieces?" "Here we are!" cried they, entering the cottage, and beginning to eat the burnt bread.

A few days passed, and again the wife told her husband to take away his children; the second journey had the same result as the first, for the girl scattered some *malain*, and so found their way home again.

Seeing that he could not live in peace with his wife, he determined to take them to a greater distance, and on a road quite unknown to them. The girl had still some malain left, which she scattered as before, but this time rain fell, and made it into a paste, which was greedily eaten up by the little birds. So they walked all day until evening, and seeing no signs of their home they climbed into a tree, and made themselves a bed amongst the branches, and slept until daybreak. When morning came, they again began their wanderings through the forest. After a time hunger seized them, and they had nothing to eat; but at last the boy cut himself a pliant stick, and taking a mesh of his sister's hair, with it and the stick made himself a bow. Soon he shot some birds, while his sister procured a fire by rubbing two pieces of wood together and setting alight some dry branches. Thus they lived for some days, until in their wanderings they met with a fox; the boy was on the point of adjusting his bow, when the fox cried "do not shoot me, and then I will give you one of my cubs, who will be useful to you," so taking the cub the boy continued his way.

Further on he encountered a she-wolf; he was again about to draw his bow when the wolf begged him to spare her life, and she would give him one of her young ones, who would be useful to him. Taking with him the young wolf, as well as the cub-fox, he went along.

Soon on his path he encountered a bear, and the same form of words and acts was gone through as with the fox and the wolf. When evening approached, the children, followed by the young animals, came suddenly on a fine palace. Entering fearlessly, the boy found in the lodge a bundle of keys; thinking that they were the keys of the palace, he took them and began to open the various doors. At length he reached a very fine carved steel door, and opening it he found there, a huge giant, bound to the wall by three iron bands. When the giant saw him he called, "youngster, bring me a jug of water, for I am dying of thirst." Instead of doing this he went in search of his sister. Giving her all the keys, he told her she might enter every room excepting the one with the steel door, but if she went into that one a misfortune would befall her.

Thus saying, he set out for the chase, followed by his three young animals.

After his departure the girl began exploring the palace, and arriving at the steel door, she said to herself, "I wonder why my brother has forbidden me this chamber! perhaps there are treasures in it which he wants for himself alone—why should he do this, seeing that I am his sister?" So trying the lock, she turned the key and entered. At sight of her, the giant cried, "maiden, bring me a jug of water, and I will be of great service to you." She went quickly, and returned with the water. After the giant had drunk it, one of his irons snapped and fell asunder.

Again the giant cried, "maiden bring me another jug of water, and you shall not have cause to repent it." Quickly she came with the water, the giant drank it eagerly, and the second band fell away.

A third time he cried, "maiden bring me but one more jug, then I shall be free, I am weary of being bound for so many years, and I will do whatsoever thou desirest." She brought him water for the third time, and after he had drunk that also, the last band snapped and fell away. The giant finding himself free, said to the maiden, "where is your brother?"

"Nenna is gone shooting," said she. "I should like to kill your brother," said he, "and to keep you to live with me here in this splendid palace, will you consent to this? Tell me so, for you have grown so dear to me, that I cannot live without you."

"How can you kill him?" said she, "he has always his fox and his wolf and his bear with him." Said the giant, "the next time he goes out, you must manœuvre to keep his beasts at home, and then I can go and swallow him up." The maiden consented, and the giant returned to his chamber.

When Nenna arrived from the forest, his sister was very loving and caressing to him; and after eating their supper they retired to rest. Next morning by daybreak, the boy was again ready to set out for the chase, but his sister fondling him, and showing signs of great affection said, "brother you amuse yourself in the forest, while I am alone all day! leave me your beasts to play with." With reluctance he consented and set off alone.

Shortly after his departure, the giant came out and bade the maiden shut up the animals securely in the room with the steel door, and to roll a heavy stone against it. Then the giant set off in pursuit of the boy, who, when he saw the giant, like a moving cloud in the distance, knew that his sister had disobeyed him, and set the giant free.

Climbing a lofty tree, he waited the approach of the giant, who was soon at the foot of the tree, calling him to come down so that he might eat him up. The boy flung him his sheep-skin cap, and called to him to gnaw at that until he had time to sing a song.

This was what he sang.

"Il! N'ande!
N'a vede!
N'a grenlu pamentului,
Ilsurelulu campului,
Ca ve pere stapanalu."

The fox heard this song, and said, "Hark! our master is in danger." "Shut your woollen ears," said the other two.

The giant had got to the last morsel of the sheepskin cap, so the boy flung one of his *opinci* (sandals) and told him to eat that also, as he had not yet finished his song.

Beginning again his song, this time the wolf heard him, but the bear said, "Be quiet I sharp ears."

By this time the sandal was devoured, and the giant in a loud voice called him to descend, but the boy flung the other sandal, and entreated time to sing one more song.

This time the bear also heard him, and said, "In truth, our master is in great peril, but how can we get to him? For we are locked in here." Said the fox, "I will make an opening," and forced himself with all his strength against the door, without success;

the same result with the wolf; but when the bear put his broad back there, the door flow open, and the stone rolled twenty paces away.

Finding themselves at liberty, the wolf said, "Shall we go like wind, or as quick as thought?"

"Like the wind!" said the bear, "for if we travel as quick as thought, we shall be breathless, and incapable of fighting when we arrive."

Like the wind they arrived to help their master. The giant, seeing their approach, transformed himself into a log of wood.

The boy cried to his beasts, "you must eat up all this wood for me, and leave for my share, only its heart and its liver."

They made no difficulty about it, so the boy, seizing the heart and the liver, returned home, to the great astonishment and vexation of his sister.

The boy made a wooden spit, and thrusting the liver and the heart on it, bade his sister prepare this food. When it was cooked he seized the spit, and striking his sister with it said, "this is because you set the giant free, and consented to my death,—do you see?"

"I see as if I were looking through a sieve!"

74

Striking her again, he said, "can you see now?"

"I see as through a mist."

Placing over her head nine casks, one above the other, and covering her completely with them, he said, "you will see clear when you have filled these nine casks with your tears;" and so he went on his way and left her to die.

THE FISHERMAN AND
THE BOYARD'S DAUGHTER.

ONCE on a time there was a good-looking fisherman, young and intelligent. Every time that he went through the court of a certain Boyard,—Mariola, the daughter of this Boyard, would call him to her, purchase his fish, and give him money to ten times its value. So much money did he gain in this way, that he began to be indifferent to its possession and yet each day Mariola would still be a customer.

On one of these occasions, while she was handing him the money, she touched his hand and gave it a squeeze; the fisherman grew as red as a beet-root, and looked down, but regaining confidence, began to give himself airs, and twirl his moustache.

Gradually they entered into conversation, and she learned that he was unmarried, and became altogether charmed with the replies she drew from him. Although he was but a fisherman, she fell desperately in love with him, and giving him a purse of gold, she bade him go and buy clothing suitable for a gentleman, and then to come back to her to shew her if they were becoming to him.

After having bought a *caftan*, and other things fit for a real Boyard, he dressed himself in them, and came to exhibit himself to Mariola.

She almost failed to recognise him, for both his carriage and dress were far above one of his station, and she could no longer restrain the love which she had for him in her heart, and gave him to understand that he might be her husband if he wished. The fisherman hesitated, knowing that he was no match for a Boyard's daughter; but finding that she still insisted, with much bashfulness, and twirling his *caciula* (cap) from hand to hand, he eventually consented.

On hearing this astounding intelligence, the Boyard was very angry, saying that a fisherman was no match for his child; but as he loved Mariola so tenderly, and seeing that her heart was set upon the marriage, eventually he consented to her prayer.

"Mariola again gave a purse of gold to her intended, bidding him buy wedding garments and all that was necessary. Shortly he presented himself, clad in a rich suit embroidered thickly with gold; Mariola conducted him to her father's presence, and they were at once affianced.

Not many days after this, the wedding took place, and they took their seats at the banquet given in honour of the occasion.

There was a rule in those days, that the newly-married pair should each eat from one lightly boiled egg; the fisherman cut a thin slice of bread, and was going to dip it into the egg, when Mariola caught his arm, saying, "No! I must eat of it first; I am a Boyard's daughter, and you are only a fisherman."

No reply did he make, but rising quietly from the table, quitted the banqueting hall, to the astonishment of many of the guests, who did not know that he had been a fisherman.

The bride was very troubled at the mistake she had made, and sat biting her lips with dismay and chagrin. Being unable to support her position, she withdrew to her bedroom, and locked herself in.

All night long sleep would not come to her, and she could only think of her absent bridegroom.

At early morning she went to her father to demand permission to go in search of her husband. Her father tried to dissuade her from taking such a step, but in vain, and she set off on her errand.

She traversed the town, the country, villages, country again—again villages; until at length, in one of these small villages, she saw him meanly dressed, and acting as servant at a wayside inn. Approaching him quickly, she began to address him, but he would not appear to know her, and continued his occupation. She entreated him only to speak one word to her, but he only shrugged his shoulders, and turned away his head.

The master of the inn seeing this interruption, called, "How is it that you interfere with my servant, and prevent his working? Don't you see that he is dumb? If you are as respectable as your appearance would show, I advise you to go away and leave him alone."

"He is not dumb," cried she, "he is my husband, and left me for a simple misunderstanding."

The villagers, who had collected around, were astonished at what she said, for she did not look like one who would be poking fun at them.

The innkeeper was also incredible, saying, that a man who was able to speak, would not remain a whole week without uttering a word. In truth, all around took him to be a mute, and used to converse with him by signs. He had already gained their goodwill, by his usefulness and good temper.

Mariola seeing that no one would believe her story, offered to make a bet, that in three days she would make her husband speak, if she were allowed always to be at his side; that if she did not succeed she would consent to be hung. This bet was accepted and legalised by the Prefect of the village.

The following day was to be the first of the trial the fisherman at the beginning of this, knew nothing of the bet, though later on, he got a whisper of it.

Mariola was constantly entreating for one little word. "My darling," she said, "I have been very wrong; I married you because I loved you, I bind myself never again, in all our life-time, to commit such a fault; soften your heart and speak one word to me." Yet no answer—only a shrug of the shoulders, as if he did not understand what she was saying.

The first day passed—came the second day; that passed too, and yet not a sound.

On the third day, Mariola began to tremble with fear, and followed the fisherman wherever he went, still begging him to speak only one word to her. He, on the other hand, fearing to be overcome by her tears, fled from her presence.

The three days have passed, all the villagers are taken up with the affair of the dumb servant at the inn, and the pretty looking girl, who had mistaken him for some one else, and brought this misfortune on herself.

The scaffold was erected, the people had congregated together to see the end of this tragedy; the officials were there, who, against their will, were bound to carry out the punishment.

The executioner approached Mariola, and led her to the scaffold, saying, that as she had failed to make the dumb man speak, she must accept the forfeit of her life.

Sighing, she turned her head once more towards her impassive husband, but seeing no yielding from him, she prepared herself to die. Loosening her hair, making the sign of the cross, she commended herself in prayer to God. All the spectators were moved at the sight. On the steps of the scaffold, with the Priest at her side, once more she turned towards the fisherman, crying, "My dear husband, pray come to my rescue, one word from you will suffice." Shaking his head, he looked in another direction.

With the noose in his hand, waited the executioner; soon he adjusted it round Mariola's pretty neck-one more minute and all would have been over; but the fisherman, stretching forth his hand, called—"Stop!"

All the people were struck with astonishment, and tears of joy rolled down their cheeks. The executioner withdrew the noose, and the fisherman, looking severely at Mariola, asked, "Will you again taunt me with being a fisherman?" With great emotion she cried, "Forgive me, my clear husband, I own my fault, and will never wound your feelings again." "Let her come down," said he, "for she is indeed my wife;" and taking her by the hand, he led her back to their home, where their life was one banquet of happiness and prosperity in future.

LEGENDS.

MANOLI.

A LEGEND OF THE 13TH CENTURY.

MONASTERY OF ARGISCH
Built by Manoli; restored 1880.

A BRILLIANT cortège winds along the banks of a river; a crowd of powerful nobles respectfully surround their Chief, whose great height and manly expression, seem to indicate him worthy of being the Commander amongst them all. In his immediate neighbourhood, nine artizans may be observed; they also yield obedience to a Chief, noted for his superior experience and knowledge.

The river below, the river whose waters roll through a country so wild, here shooting up into cascades, and there falling back murmuring on the pointed rocks worn and sharpened by their beatings; lower down, flowing evenly along—sometimes subdued, sometimes in revolt—emblematic alike of life, will, impatience, and human resignation;—this river is the Argis, and the country through which it flows is called *Lesser Wallachia*.

The Chief whom we see surrounded by his nobles, mounted on their splendid horses, with gorgeous trappings, is *Radu the Black*, Prince of the country, and founder of the Principality.

This brilliant cavalcade is in reality a pious pilgrimage, in search of a suitable site, to be consecrated by the erection of a Monastery, unequalled for beauty of position, and richness of design.

This is also why, amongst so illustrious a company are to be found the nine masons, headed by the master hand of all the masons—the renowned *Manoli*.

A young shepherd comes in sight, playing on his flute, a Doïna (National wail) of his country.

"Shepherd," cried Radu, stopping him, "thou must often with thy flocks have explored the banks of the Argis; tell me, hast thou never seen a wall hidden amongst the green brushwood of the nut trees?"

"Yes, Prince, I have seen a wall which was begun to be built, and my dogs howled at it, as if they had been howling for a death."

"Right," said the Prince, with satisfaction, "it is there that our Monastery shall rise;" then calling Manoli and his masons, "Listen," he said, "I wish you to build me an edifice, so noble and beautiful, that its equal shall never be found, neither in the present nor in the future. I promise to you all, treasures, titles, and estates, which shall make you equals with the Boyards of my court. I promise, on the honour of a Prince, and you know you may rely on my promises. Wait 1 don't thank me yet! My word is sacred, and again I say, what I promise I always carry out; if you *do not succeed, I will have you walled up living*, in the foundation of the Monastery, which shall be built by cleverer hands than yours."

Terror, and ambition! two great incentives for all men! So the masons get quickly to work; they measure the ground; they dig the soil; and soon a majestic wall begins to rise.

Satisfied with their work, and certain of success, they fall asleep and dream of the lands, and treasures, and titles, which their skilfulness is to bring them.

Morning comes, the golden rays of the sun dart over the waters of the Argis; the cool morning air, and the desire to continue their work— only interrupted for needful repose—arouse the masons; they seize their tools, and walk quickly to recommence their labours; but, alas! that wall, those solid foundations, all, all, during the night, had crumbled and disappeared.

Instead of sitting down and complaining, the masons recommenced their task; they think of the Prince, and of his oath, and they Work and tremble, and tremble and work.

At length, at the end of the day—a long summer's clay, they have repaired the terrible disaster, and when evening comes, they again seek repose.

Again morning, and again sunlight reveals the crumbled walls!

In despair, the workmen recommence; for has not the Prince sworn his terrible oath? But when night comes, they no longer dream of treasures and titles, but of the terrible chastisement which awaits them.

When they again awake, all is ruin, and this happens four times to them.

The fourth night, notwithstanding his anxiety, Manoli sleeps, and he dreams a strange and terrible dream. He awakes, and calls his comrades. "Listen," he says, "to what has been told to me while I was asleep. A voice whispered to me that all our work will be in vain; that each night, the work of each day will be destroyed, unless we wall up, living, in our edifice, the first woman, be she wife or sister, who in the early morning comes to bring our food."

The prospects of the honours which the construction of the Monastery was to bring them; the riches and titles with which their work was to be recompensed—decided the workmen, and they each swore a solemn oath, to wall up while living, be she sister, or wife, the first woman who should come amongst them next day.

Morning arrived, clear and pure, as if it would not light on one despairing heart. Manoli anxiously looks into the distance, his oath strikes him with terror; but he is ambitious, and why should he refuse to sacrifice some one, to insure his own safety, and the success of his labour? Looking at it in this light, the engagement becomes a sacred duty; it is humane even, to secure the safety of several, at the price of one, and Manoli begins to regard the proceeding as heroic.

Yet he is restless, and gets on a hillock to look around him, to see still further; he oven mounts a scaffolding, and his eyes scan fearfully the surrounding plain.

Distant, far distant, he sees something advancing. Who comes in such haste? In truth, it is a woman, careful and diligent, bringing the early morning meal to the man she loves. See, with light quick step, she comes nearer and nearer, she is recognised. It is the beautiful Flora, the wife of Manoli, Everything disappears from Manoli's sight, the sun is dark, and swollen; instead of light, there is the darkness of the tomb.

He falls on his knees, and, joining his hands, calls, Oh, Lord, God; open the cataracts of Heaven, shower on the earth torrents of water, turn the streamlets into lakes, oh, Merciful Saviour, that my wife may not be able reach me here!" Did God listen to his prayer? Shortly clouds covered the sky, and heavy rain began to fall, but Flora continued her way. Was not her husband waiting? What mattered these obstacles?

Against stream and torrent, she still advances, and Manoli watching her, again kneels, joins his bands, and cries, "Oh, my God, send a wind to twist and tear up the plantains, to overthrow the mountains, and to force my wife to return to the valley!"

The wind rises and whistles in the forest, uproots the plantains, to overthrow mountains, yet Flora only hastens more quickly to reach her husband and at length arrives at the fatal spot. Then the masons tremble at the sight, but tremble with joy.

While Manoli, grief stricken, takes his wife in his arms and says, "Listen, my dear, to amuse ourselves, we are going to pretend to build you up in these walls, it will be I, who will place you there, so remain very quiet."

Flora laughingly consented, for she loved Manoli and had full confidence in him. Manoli sighed heavily, but though sighing, began to build the wall, which already reaches to the ankles of Flora—to her knees—higher and higher. Flora laughs no longer, but, seized with terror, cries, "Manoli, oh, Manoli, leave off this cruel joking, the wall presses on me, it will crush me,"

Manoli is silent, but works on, the wall still rises, and is now level with her waist.

Again she cries, "Manoli! Manoli! stay your hand; soon I shall no longer see you; I love you so; you are sacrificing me, and yet you say you love me too."

Manoli works on, and to console himself, thinks, "Shortly I shall hear no longer her complaining; suffering is not so bad, when one does not witness it."

The work proceeds—the wall rises even to her eye-brows—at length she is hid from sight entirely. Manoli moves away, but still hears the faint moaning voice of his wife. "Manoli, Manoli, the wall is pressing on me, and my life is dying out."

* * * * *

The day was magnificent on which the Prince came to kneel and give thanks at the beautiful Monastery the best proportioned, and the finest in style and grandeur which had ever been built. The master masons, Manoli amongst them, swelling with pride, waited, at the top of the scaffolding, the visit, the praise, and the recompense of Radii their Prince.

"Well, is it true," said the Prince, "that you could never imagine, or construct, an edifice more splendid than this? Can no other Sovereign signalise his power and his wealth by a finer building than this?"

The masons inflamed with pride and emulation, cried with a triumphant air, "Know, Prince, that we are the Master Masons, whose science and skill is unrivalled: we might be able, even, to create a greater work than this."

The Prince turned aside with a wicked smile.

"Wait up here for me," he said, "I will go down to fully examine the edifice from below, and I will come up again and make my observations to you." Hurrying from the scaffolding, he gave a quick sign, and command to the people below, who speedily knocked away, props, poles, and planks, and the masons fell from the great height to an instantaneous death. Manoli, alone caught at a projecting carving, and passing from one to another, would soon have reached the ground, but there came from the wall which he was touching, the cry, "Manoli, Manoli, the cold wall is pressing on me, my body is crushed, and my life is dying out." At this sound, Manoli, turns giddy and faint, and falls to the earth.

On the spot where he fell, there springs a fountain of clear sparkling water, but its taste is salt and bitter, as the tears which are shed in Roumania, even now, when any one relates the sorrows and the sacrifice of Flora, the wife of Manoli.

THE FORTRESS OF POINARII.

I.

CONSTANTINOPLE had fallen into the hands of the Turks, and disorder reigned in the Roumanian Principalities, mainly occasioned by the pretenders to the thrones.

In Moldavia, Stephen, who was afterwards surnamed the *Great*, made war against Aron, the murderer of his father, Bogdan, and putting to flight Berendei, who disputed his power, remained sole master of the crown, which he was destined to wear so gloriously for more than 40 years.

In Wallachia, Vlad the 5th, son of Vlad the Devil, cut his way to the throne, sabre in hand, and maintained it by the greatest terrorism and tyranny.

He formed a numerous army, cut off the heads of more than 500 Boyards, who would not join his party, caused to be massacred on one pretext or another, more than 20,000 men; and burned alive, in a barn, 400 Hungarians, whom he ordered to be shut up there, and who were living in his country.

These exploits accomplished, he crossed the Carpathians, and went into Transylvania, set fire to the four corners of the town of Brasov (Cronstadt), and seizing a number of the inhabitants, caused them to be empaled in front of the St. Jacob Church.

He then returned to his Principality, feared even more than death itself by the people, and having acquired the stigma to his name—Vlad the Empaler!

II.

Had this tyrant contented himself with empaling Hamzi, the Pasha of Widdin, in the midst of the Turks, whom with Hamzi he had made prisoners; if his brutal rage, and his thirst for blood, had been exercised against the enemies of his country, that might have passed; there would have been some excuse—some extenuation for his senseless cruelty.

Vlad the Empaler, was an exception—monstrous, even in those barbaric times, which God in his malediction, does sometimes send as a curse to his people.

Vlad was created for the part he played; he hated foreigners! he hated the Boyards! he hated the people! He massacred, empaled, killed, without distinction for his own pleasure and security.

III.

Vlad waged a war of extermination against the Turks augmented his army, and raised many fortresses his coffers were empty, and he laid heavy taxes upon his people. Poor and rich alike Must all contribute to give him money. But the people revolted, all—great and small—refused the heavy impositions which he wished to force upon them. Vlad drew back an instant, full of rage, and swearing to himself to be terribly revenged, when the suitable moment presented itself.

It was not long in coming!

In Tergoviste, all is joy! It is 1470, and Easter Day! Every one is out in holiday attire, wending their way towards the church, or walking about the streets; the bells are ringing, and everything seems joyous under this bright blue sky. Vlad, alone, is sombre and silent. He has not forgotten that once he was obliged to bend to the will of his subjects, and dreams continually of vengeance.

IV.

All at once he rises, and calls around him his Captains, and gives his instructions to them in a low voice.

Soon, armed soldiers are assembled in the Castle Court; they leave by detachments, in silence, spread themselves along the streets of Tergoviste, close in the public places, and surround the churches. All who were outside, laughing, or inside, at the foot of the altar,—those who smiled, and those who prayed, all found themselves in a circle of iron, seized, thrown pell mell into the enclosure of the palace. Men, women, children, without distinction of age, sex, or condition were there-mute and terror-stricken, awaiting some great and inevitable calamity. Vlad regarded them with a mocking laugh; his eye, as it glanced over them, was that of a wild beast which has its prey in its power, and rejoicing at the nameless horror which he saw depicted on all their faces; he decided to make them acquainted with his will.

V.

The Empaler had been one day hunting along the banks of the river Argis, and had remarked on Mount Albina, a position which he considered admirable. It was an immense rock, on the top of which was a capacious platform, but so high that it seemed to touch the clouds.

Vultures, and birds of prey, alone, inhabited it, and the tumultuous waves of the Argis, beat continually at its base.

Vlad conceived the design, there to build a fortress, which would be impregnable; but for that, he needed money, and his people had refused it to him! Then he came to another resolution, and with this he now made his prisoners acquainted.

"You would not give me the money I needed," he said, "well, keep it! I will not have you killed to chastise you for your revolt, but I condemn you all, just as you are, to build with your own hands a Fortress on the top of Mount Albina. I wish it to be the largest, the best built, and the most impregnable of all which I possess. You will not leave the mountain until all is finished. My soldiers, have the right of life and death over you, to force you to carry out my instructions."

VI.

No sooner said than done, and these unfortunate creatures, young and old, huddled together in gala dress, without saying good-bye to those who were happy enough to have remained at home, were conducted, like criminals, to the bank of the river, at the foot of the mountain. Then, after making footpaths, almost perpendicular in the mountain, they gained the platform, and were surrounded by their stern guardians, exposed to every change in the atmosphere, and to nameless tortures.

Masons, stonecutters, carpenters, blacksmiths, all those who knew any trade, set to work. Those who hitherto had been brought up in luxury, mixed mortar, women chipped stones, young girls carried water, and even children were set to work suitable for their age. One might see at the top and the sides of the mountain, a human ant-hill, always in motion, occupied in this atrocious labour.

Sun, rain, and wind, blackened their faces; their clothes hung in shreds; their features haggard and careworn, some eyes burning with rage, others with the submission of despair. These are no longer human beings, but machines, stupified by sorrow, and no longer able oven to implore God above, to send down his maledictions on the tyrant. Still their work progressed, and soon this *citta dolente*, was completed.

Vlad arrives, and after looking at it with the minutest attention, seeing that it equalled his expectations, in his clemency, sent back to their dwellings all that remained of these miserable workpeople.

On the banks of the Argis, not far from Stoieneste, may still be seen the ruins of what is called in the country, *the cursed ruins of the Fortress of Poinarii.*

THE GENTLE SHEPHERD.

ON the edge of a mountain, lovely as the entrance to paradise, see, coming along, and descending toward the valley, three flocks of young lambs, driven by three young shepherds; one is an inhabitant of the plains of Moldau, the other is Hungarian, the third is from the Vrantcha Mountain. The Hungarian and the Vranchian have held counsel together, and have resolved that at sunset they will kill their companion, on account of his riches, for he owns more horned sheep than they do, his horses are better trained than theirs, and his dogs more vigorous. Yet, for three days past, there is in his flock a fair young sheep, with white silky wool, who will no longer eat the tender grass of the prairie, and moans all day long.

"My poor little sheep, you who were so fat and well! how is it that for three days you have done nothing but groan and moan? don't you like the prairie grass, or are you ill, my dear little lamb?"

"Oh, my beloved shepherd, lead thy flock to that thicket, there will be grass for us, and shade for thee; master, dear master! call near you without delay, one of your best and strongest dogs, for the Hungarian and the Vranchian have resolved to kill you at sunset!"

"Dear little sheep of the mountains, if thou art a prophetess, if it is written that I am to die in the bosom of these pastures, thou wilt tell the Hungarian and the Vranchian to bury me near this spot, not far from this enclosure, so that I may always be near you, my beloved lambs,—either here, or behind the shepherd's hut, so that I may always hear the voice of my faithful dogs. Thou wilt tell them this, and thou wilt place at the foot of nay grave a little flute of elm wood, with its accents of love;

another of bone, with its harmonious sounds; another of reeds, with its passionate notes; and when the wind blows across their pipes bringing out plaintive music, then my flock will assemble round my tomb, and weep for me, tears of blood."

"Take care thou dost not tell them of my murder! tell them I have married a beautiful Queen, that at the moment of our union, a star fell, that the sun and moon together held the crown over my head, that I exist no longer for them. But if ever thou meetest, if ever thou comest near, a poor old mother, running across the fields, weeping and asking, 'who amongst you have seen a young shepherd, with face as fair as milk, with moustache yellow as ripe corn, with waist so slight that it would pass through a ring, with raven hair, and eyes like mulberries?'—then my little sheep, take pity on her, and tell her that I have married a daughter of the King who lives at the entrance of paradise, but say nothing to her of the falling star!" Here ends the fragment.

HISTORIC TALES.

DEATH OF CONSTANTIN
II. BRANCOVAN.

MODERN history presents no greater catastrophe, nor one more nobly endured than that of the death of Brancovan. Already this Prince had reigned twenty-five years; an unparalleled event in Wallachian history.

Under this long reign, great ameliorations had been made in every branch of the administration. Laws were regarded, order and security exercised a salutary influence, agriculture flourished, commerce prospered; luxury was introduced in the towns, comfort in the country, magnificence at Court. Added to this material prosperity, was joined the elements of intellectual culture.

From the commencement of his reign, Brancovan, seeing the rising tide of Ottoman oppression submerge, one by one, the last traces of Roumanian independence, meditated, like some of his illustrious predecessors, the absolute freedom of his country.

On the other hand the Sultans, their Viziers, and their minions, contemplated its complete subjugation, in order to profit without obstacle or control, by *"the garden and granary of Stamboul."*

Both the intelligence and the resources of Brancovan were equal to the great work which he projected. Knowing thoroughly the character of the Turk, possessing immense wealth, wisely accumulated from year to year, notwithstanding the extortions, and the endless exactions of the Suzerain Power, politician enough to interest both the Empire and Russia in his cause, he could, according to all the rules of human prudence, calculate on success. Unhappily, circumstances were against him. The peace of Karlovitz, rendered help from the Empire hopeless, so he looked with confidence towards Russia, which Peter the Great was then making celebrated in Europe; but the jealousy of Cantimir, Prince of Moldavia, and the treaty of the Pruth, broke down all his clever combinations.

The Sublime Porte, informed by its spies of what was taking place at Bucharest, and of the projects of Brancovan, resolved to depose him, to seize his person, and to have him brought to Constantinople, to do with him according to its pleasure. But Brancovan was so rich, that his gold made him friends even in the heart of the Divan; he sent the Viziers, the Sultan even, such magnificent presents, that they postponed his ruin.

He believed he had surmounted the danger, and credulous in his good fortune, like many other successful men, he remained deaf to the warnings of his friends, the entreaties of his family, even to the presentiments of one of his daughters, who, dying in the flower of her age, before expiring, had the frightful vision of the martyrdom of her father and brothers.

Accusations arriving from Bucharest, complaints covered with false Signatures, hurried on the catastrophe. On March 22, 1714, Capidji Moustafa Aga arrived at Bucharest, bearing the firman of dethronement. He was introduced into the palace with an escort of twelve *Tchohodars*, secretly armed, with poignards and pistols, and solemnly deposed Brancovan in the throne room, throwing upon his shoulders the black veil, and pronouncing the terrible word *Mazil* (deposed).

The Turkish Envoy set off again quickly for Constantinople, taking with him, as prisoners, Constantin Brancovan and his family.

On his arrival at Stamboul, the captives were conducted to the castle of the seven towers, a state prison celebrated in Turkish annals for the multitude of its bloody tragedies. It was the threshold of agony, and agony did not keep them long in waiting.

The Sultan, Achmet III. himself presided at the slaughter, and the unfortunate Brancovan, his soul elevated by the sublimest Christian sentiments, washed, with his blood, any stains that might have been in his life.

By a refinement of savage cruelty, after having tortured the father in the presence of his children, before the father's eyes they cut off the heads, one by one, of his four sons. Each time that the head of these young Princes fell, the Sultan offered to pardon Brancovan, if he would embrace Mahometanism; the heroic father pointed towards heaven, and the slaughter continued. When Brancovan's turn arrived to lay his head on the block, he said with resignation: "If my death comes from God, as a punishment for my sins, His will be done; if it comes from my enemies, may Heaven forgive them." And, deaf to the voice of the Sultan, who still bade him deny his Christ, and with eyes raised to heaven, stood still as a statue! Achmet gave a sign, bright steel glimmered, a jet of blood covered the wall, and the soul of the good old. man had rejoined those of his sons.

There remained yet a sixth victim—a poor little child, the only grandson of Brancovan. Mad with terror, the child hid himself in the Caftan of Bostandjibachi, who, overwhelmed with benefits by the murdered Princes, much against his will, had been forced to be present at all these atrocities.

He had the hardihood to take the boy in his arms, and to cast an imploring look at the Sultan. The ferocious Achmet, regarding the child, and then the five corpses, made a sign of pardon, and so the last heir of this illustrious family was saved.

The heads of the five martyrs, stuck on lances, were carried about in the streets of Stamboul, preceded by heralds, crying, "this is the end of traitors." Their bodies were thrown into the sea, but at nightfall some Christian boatmen drew them out, and they were piously buried in a little Island in the Sea of Marmora.

The domains of Brancovan were confiscated, and his almost fabulous riches were shared between the Sultan, and the instigators of his ruin.

This touching and terrible catastrophe, made a profound impression not only in Wallachia and Moldavia, but throughout Europe. Transmitted from generation to generation, it has passed from history to legend, which is recounted from the Danube to the Carpathians, in cities and in villages, and at the modest firesides of the Roumanian peasants. The native poet, Alexandri, has made it the subject of one of his most beautiful and touching ballads.

THE MOTHER OF STEPHEN THE GREAT.

IT was not alone in Sparta that Lacedemonians were to be found—not Rome alone, which could pride herself on her heroic-hearted matrons!

In 1476, Etienne le Grand was reigning Prince of Moldavia, and the Turks were waging heavy war against that Principality. The Sultan, Mahomet, wished to reconquer the provinces of Kilia and Ackerman, and he carried devastation and terror throughout the country. Etienne rushed forward to encounter him. Etienne the glorious! Etienne the vanquisher! has sounded his war trumpet, and from all surrounding parts his valiant warriors have joined him.

The meeting took place at *Valea Alba*—the white valley—on July 26th, 1476. The Moldavians performed prodigies of valour, they struggled like lions, and at one time were almost victorious, but Mahomet, furious and with flaming eyes, flung himself into their midst, and overpowered and crushed them by his superior force. Etienne, thrown from his horse, wounded, and in despair, escaped with the remnant of his army, and with drew to the mountains. Night, sombre and sad, is on them; a cold fierce wind freezes their very blood. At length, Etienne, harrassed and suffering, arrives before his castle, and orders his trumpet to be sounded.

* * * * *

In this old fortress, built on the side of a mountain, the mother of the Prince keeps watch as a sentinel of honour. Voichitza, the young wife of the Prince, is also there, sweet and suave as a white carnation, sighing for her glorious and much-loved lord, who returns not from the combat.

The Princess, her mother-in-law, consoles and cheers her. The clock had just struck midnight, when Voichitza heard the fanfare of the trumpet, and the knocking at the gate. She knows it is her husband, and her heart goes out to him. Both the Princesses rise quickly, and goon the voice of him whom they love cries from the darkness:

"It is I, thy son, dear mother, I, thy son! I am wounded in battle, the struggle has been too strong for us, and my little army is devastated. Open the gates, for the Turks are surrounding us, the wind is piercing, and my wounds are painful."

Voichitza rushes to the window, but her mother-in-law holds her back, and bidding her remain where she is, descends the stairs, orders the Castle gates to be opened, and appears before her son, tall, majestic, severe—the absolute personification of dignity and grandeur.

"*What* do you say, *Stranger? My Etienne* is far away I his arm is sowing death and annihilation. *I* am his mother, he is *my* son! If *you* are *really* Etienne, *I* am not *your* mother! If heaven does not wish to make my last days sorrowful, and if you are really Etienne, you will not enter here, vanquished, against my will. Fly to the battle field! die for your country! your tomb shall be flower strewn!" And closing the door, she re-mounted the stairs; and, calm and serene, consoled and wiped away the tears of the young Princess Voichitza.

* * * * *

Etienne, repulsed by her whom he loved so much—Etienne, whom the God of battles seemed to have abandoned—Etienne, the valiant, blessed his mother, and sent through the night air a tender kiss to his young wife. Then, sounding a furious fanfare, he rode away, with the remnant of his followers, into obscurity. He caused fires to be lighted on the hills, and at this sign of call to arms, soldiers seemed to spring forth in every direction.

Etienne has once more an army, and they turn in pursuit of the enemy, decided either to die, or become victorious.

The soldiers of Mahomet had devastated and sacked the whole of Moldavia, and were preparing to return with their plunder into their own country. Etienne and his men came up with them near to the banks of the Danube, surprised them, and cut them in pieces. The remnant of the Turkish troops fled across the river in the greatest confusion, leaving their plunder behind them.